AMERICA'S CHILD

A Woman's Journey
through the Radical Sixties

a memoir by

SUSAN SHERMAN

CURBSTONE PRESS

Printed in Canada on acid-free paper
Cover design: Susan Sherman
Cover photos used by permission of the author.

This book was published with the support of
the Connecticut Commission on Culture and
Tourism, the Connecticut State Legislature
through the Office of Policy & Management,
and donations from many individuals.
We are grateful for this support.

Library of Congress Cataloging-in-Publication Data

Sherman, Susan, 1939-
  America's child : a woman's journey through the radical sixties / by
Susan Sherman. — 1st ed.
    p. cm.
  ISBN 978-1-931896-35-1 (pbk. : alk. paper)
  1. Sherman, Susan, 1939- 2. Poets, American—20th century—
Biography. I. Title.

  PS3569.H434Z46 2007
  811'.54—dc22

                                        2007022399

published by
CURBSTONE PRESS 321 Jackson St. Willimantic, CT 06226
      phone: 860-423-5110   e-mail: info@curbstone.org
                    www.curbstone.org

Always you will live here, close as the blood that flows through the veins of my hand. As I walk into the desert. Father, mother, country. The dream clutched tight to my body, like a lover.

Contents

CUBA AND AFTER, 1968-1971:
The Movement & Other Revelations

HOME:
New York City, 2006

July 12, 2004. New York City. I sit in a theater crowded with people watching "The Control Room," a documentary focusing on the controversial Arab network Al-Jazeera. We are bombarded with scenes of devastation—children with bloody limbs, remnants of burned-out homes, people's lives destroyed as the result of American intervention in Iraq. An Al-Jazeera commentator turns toward the camera and grimaces sarcastically during a speech by George W. Bush. The audience laughs. Sitting in that darkened room, I am transported back to another time almost four decades earlier. A time I never expected to relive...

I am in Havana, Cuba. It is 1969. I am sitting in an auditorium filled with Vietnamese students watching a Cuban film documenting the American bombing of North Vietnam. Bombs cut the air, fill the screen. I wait, anxiously anticipating the inevitable explosion that must follow. But the impact is silent, signaled only by spirals of dust rising in slow motion from the earth. A silence more ominous, more deadly, than any sound.

I stare straight ahead, rigid, wondering if they realize I am American, wondering if surreptitiously they are looking at me, gauging my reaction.

Then, when an American plane is finally shot down, shouts and cheers go up across the room, and the small group of Americans sitting beside me joins in. But I can't cheer. The contradictions are too painful, too vivid. I can only sit and take it in—in silence.

Take it all in, deep inside.

BERKELEY 1958 - 1961

2478 TELEGRAPH AVENUE

Each important place in a person's life always seems to relate to one special sense, has something unique you can identify and remember it by. In Berkeley it was smell. The smell of eucalyptus after dark. A night scent carried by a night breeze. Imagine, if you can, the aroma of a Mexican *flauta* (chicken or cheese wrapped with tortilla, delicately fried, smeared with guacamole and sour cream, take-out 40¢) washed down with a pint of beer while you sit by an old iron stove built in 1919—a brass plate attesting to its age on the oven door—hiding your food from Thornbranch, a cat so-named because as a kitten he was rescued from a paper bag a junkie had tied him in, swinging him round and round his head, so that for months whenever someone moved too near, he would jump on them and cling like a thorn branch, kitten claws clutched into clothes, legs, whatever was exposed and close.

Imagine touching the hot burning streets in October—summer being mostly cool—or surviving the months in winter when there is continual rain, the sky looking like an inverted gray bowl on the horizon.

If you can imagine these things, then you might be able to sense the Berkeley of the late Fifties and early Sixties, even before the free speech movement, echoing to the political organizing call of SLATE, the first independent coalition to challenge the traditionally conservative student government and bring it into the arena of activism and human rights.

This was the Berkeley of poets, political activists, jazz musicians, students, and just hangers on. The Berkeley of revelation and division, of cheap wine and hamburgers and stolen food, of old movies (two shows a night and three on Sundays), of the House Un-American Activities Committee

1

demonstrations, of bigotry and idealism, of violence always just beneath the surface, of first sex and first love—two very different events.

Of a history even then.

Across the bay in San Francisco, North Beach was crowded with people listening to the revival of an ancient tradition in poetry, spoken poetry, which had been left in the trail of the Beats and the "San Francisco Renaissance." What Allen Ginsberg and Gregory Corso, what Helen Adam, Lawrence Ferlinghetti, and Robert Duncan had created around them was a world. A world you pressed against the way a child presses against a candy store window. The way I had pressed against the window of an old café in Berkeley the year before and had wanted and been afraid to and then finally, tentatively entered, to find I had entered a place of birth, like the glass mirrors in a fun house, always leading forward, a series of windows really, a new kind of space. Because the whole search in the late Fifties and early Sixties was a search for new forms, for new ways of seeing and feeling.

To discover the world you have known since childhood is not the only world is probably the most important discovery in a person's life, because it is to discover the possibility of not one, but many alternatives. It is to discover the possibility of choice.

How clearly I remember my first impression of Berkeley the day I arrived. It was as if I had been thrown back to my recognition at the age of ten of physically changing size, coming home after a summer away and finding things mysteriously smaller, familiar things like a favorite book, a placemat, a milk bottle. But now it was different, it was houses and streets, cars and people, that seemed to have shrunk in size. A second recognition, this time at eighteen, of growing at the expense of things outside.

"Stop for a minute will you, I want to get out of the car."

I suddenly felt suffocated, as if the buildings on each side of me were walls that would momentarily start closing in. I panicked. I didn't want to go back home, had nowhere else to go, but if I didn't get out of the car immediately, I felt I would burst.

"What's the matter with you? We're going to be late."

The voice coming from the front seat of the car seemed disembodied, urgent. It only magnified my sense of dislocation, of needing to stand outside, quietly, for a moment, to establish my space.

"Please, just for a minute."

The car slammed to a stop. The driver obviously afraid I was going to be sick.

There is nothing worse than a strange city, where you know no one, have no road marks to hang on to, no favorite street where you know each turn, which leads with total predictability in any direction you choose to go.

By 1959, the city had assumed normal proportions. I had fitted myself comfortably into my new surroundings. 2478 Telegraph Avenue: a rented room (shared bathroom, shared kitchen, shared living room—at night another bedroom.) A magic place to my uninitiated eyes. And even now, decades later, the traces of that magic remain. As the world of childhood, of Los Angeles in the Forties and Fifties, simultaneously receding into the background and coming into focus, started to also assume a shape I could recognize and finally begin to understand. As I became aware of sound, smell, touch, my own form and the form of the world around me. As my life began to take on meaning, a consciousness, a physicality missing before. As I began to slowly separate things out, identify them, give them names. As I began to identify myself, name myself, separate myself out from the world around me. Assume a posture mine alone.

2478 Telegraph Avenue: a rooming house with two "suites" and a single room on the second floor, six or more single rooms on the third. The first floor was occupied by a grocery store. My room was on the second floor in a three-room complex bordering a large kitchen which I shared with two other students—Diane Wakoski, a Berkeley poet, and La Monte Young, the musician with whom she lived—and the occupants of the small room in the front of the building nominally connected to our "suite," Max and his wife, whose name I never did learn. They were very private, almost never left their room, and were more like rumors than real people.

A large room with a gray wooden door, my bedroom had a big bay window where I set my bed, jamming it carefully against three large window panes overlooking the street. The very place which a decade later would become an anti-war center, first destroyed by a bomb and then later, and with much more finality, by a wrecking truck, to be turned into a parking lot, where on Sundays peddlers would gather to sell beads and moccasins, pottery and tofu pies.

The building had a reputation. It was the place where artists lived. The *de facto* building managers, two painters from New York, Donna and Carl Worth, lived down the hall. I would not understand until years later when I moved to New York why they had three locks on their door which were carefully checked each time they left the house. Not only didn't I have locks on my own door, most of the time it was just left open.

I try to recall her, this Susan of more than four decades ago. Try to conjure her face in my mind. I find myself as frozen as she was so long ago, looking around her at new streets, new people, smelling new smells, even the air striking at the surfaces of her skin, new. I look into the mirror, turn my face from side to side. It doesn't help, is a distraction really. Of course, she would resemble me, being me, but resemblance means little. A lesson I learned the hard way, returning to Berkeley in the late Seventies to find it alien, even though outwardly it still looked much the same.

I pick up a photograph of myself from that time. How

conventionally we dressed, even as rebels, in relationship to the way we, all of us, dress today. I am wearing a skirt, have short brown hair, am sitting on the edge of a wide wooden table. My face looks so young. I reach toward it, touch it, as if to reach toward myself, as if to physically hold myself, those evenings, why is it always the evenings I remember best?

Poetry readings at night in a darkened apartment, a candle passed from poet to poet as we took our turn to read. A row of empty wine bottles, blue and white ceramic, converted into candlesticks, lining the borders of the walls. The dozens of men I slept with as part of the "sexual revolution." Those nights rising from a strange man's bed, seeing a stranger's shoes, underclothes, on the floor beside my own. Or sometimes at dawn, dressing and leaving quietly before they could awaken. Walking the empty streets to my own bed, my own place.

I often think years are not cumulative, somehow they are passed one after the other, like steps—in order to advance to the next, it being necessary to leave the last behind. That is why it is crucial now for me to reach across the years, to somehow communicate with that young woman, that self, who was once me. To make that connection.

Not that I would want to send her advice, or warn her— if that could somehow miraculously be possible. What good would it do and what alternative could I even now recommend?

Perhaps it is really I who am looking for something from her. Something I have forgotten only she can tell me, only she can make me understand.

BLOODLETTING

Those years in Berkeley I felt the way you feel traveling in a foreign country—constantly staring at small treasures you pick up along the way just to convince yourself, yes, you really *are* there. The feeling of being slightly out of contact, slightly out of touch. Berkeley was, after all, unfamiliar territory. A world where people talked about dragons and witches, read Tarot cards, and lived the unknown and unseen. It was the beginning of a realization that would finally come to me years later in New York—being an artist often means being literally two people, one constantly scrutinizing and commenting on the other. The silent observation of living detail, including yourself.

At its worst this feeling of disassociation manifested itself in the inability to communicate or connect. Sitting to one side, as I had trained myself to do as a child, hoping no one would notice me, that I could stay outside the chaos, the violence, that was my home. A helpful habit until one day it leapt out of control: the aversion to being touched, the inability to speak.

I felt this most often those first few months in the new home I shared with Diane and La Monte, people who were virtual strangers to me, but would become pivotal in future years. Now my silence came from being new, from wanting to see and learn. Not that I felt completely comfortable—I felt awkward, conventional, ashamed of my innocence.

It bothered me for anyone to know at twenty I had never slept with a man, the acceptable condition for a "nice girl" where I came from, but not here, where people laughed and made jokes about "virgins."

Being a virgin became the symbol to me of the world I so desperately wanted to leave and could only leave by becoming a part of this new world. So at an ordinary party on an ordinary night no more than two weeks after I moved into Telegraph Avenue, no more than three months after my twentieth birthday, I decided to act.

It was a warm night. Everything seemed stuck together. Even the people at the party seemed somehow glued to each other. I found this reassuring. It made me feel secure. I decided before the night was out I would no longer be embarrassed by my inexperience, no longer unknowingly be the butt of jokes and snide remarks. I had a couple of drinks—Vodka, first with Ginger Ale and then straight—and chose a teaching assistant in economics, a tall man, probably over six foot four. I liked tall men, although later I would joke that picking out one this big as my first lover was probably a mistake.

I walked over to him quietly, initiated a conversation. We began to dance. Before the hour was out, we were kissing passionately on the couch, and I had decided to take him home. All I had was a cot. I hadn't had a chance to buy a bed yet, it would have to do. As we were going up the stairs to my room, I informed him I had never slept with a man before.

He stopped, looked a little startled. I was surprised how unemotional I felt. How removed. I had been far more nervous about far less important things.

"Would you prefer not to come up? Is it all right?"

"Oh, no, not at all. You just startled me." He was obviously delighted.

"Although you really should be more careful. You never know who you could run into at a party. You're lucky it was me."

We went into my room, undressed, and he proceeded to perform with all the skill of a fledgling academic, accompanying each step with a comprehensive lecture on how a condom was properly fitted—at least a half inch of empty space had to be left at the top—why it was essential for it to be used correctly, finally climbing on top of me with little effort and little grace. It all seemed to happen so fast.

There was no fear, just a kind of bewilderment, and then a few moments of really intense pain.

"Am I hurting you? I'm sorry, just hold on. It will be over soon."

He got off me, switched me to my side, explained this was another "popular position" that was sometimes more comfortable, and proceeded to go through the motions again. It hurt less this time, although I was beginning to feel quite sore, and when he left I was glad to see him go, grateful he "couldn't spend the night." I was tired and needed to be alone and think.

I continued to spot blood on and off for the next two days. I felt older, not unlike the first day I had started my period. Like I had passed through a certain rite. A ritual of blood. I was disappointed, but hadn't expected much really. Had oddly had no romantic notions at all. That night was just something I felt I had to do.

Between him and me now, at least for me, there was a kind of bond. Enough that, even though I really had no desire to ever sleep with him again, I felt genuinely betrayed when I learned, bumping into him accidentally one day on the street, he was married, and "couldn't see me again."

I enjoyed finding myself suddenly attractive to men, having three or four or more of them constantly courting me. Up to that point I had never really considered myself the kind of woman who was popular with men. It wasn't looks, I just didn't have the kind of sexuality, the flirtatiousness, that appealed to the boys in high school or in my first two years in college. I had had dates, had gone steady, at one point actually almost considered marriage, but I was pronounced too serious, too smart, and told it would never work. Now, it seemed I had found men who liked my spirit, brains, and, I had to be honest about it, the fact I was available and would sleep with them. I hardly ever went out with them more than once or twice. Some of the more sensitive ones felt some kind of lingering bond, a sentiment I now rarely returned—which I found made me even more desirable. Most of them treated me well, although there was a surprising amount of impotence, and some experiences were disagreeable and came very close to rape. I slept with all of them, finding that easier finally than saying no.

Around this time, I began to have a recurring dream. I dreamt I was paralyzed—awake, but unable to move or speak. I was convinced when I closed my eyes I could see through my eyelids, could note every detail of the room around me. I awoke many nights in the middle of the night, sweating, forcing myself from sleep, afraid to return to a state of unconsciousness, of helplessness. Sometimes a voice intruded, sometimes laughter. Most often it was just me, alone, in the night.

I wondered if that was what death was like. Why so many people feared being buried alive.

Except for nightmares, I don't remember being afraid those years at Berkeley. At least not of new things. Things for which I had no reference. There was the fear of going home. A fear of the past. Fear of my stepfather. Sleeping for a whole year in my early teens with a baseball bat by my side. Making sure I was never alone in the house. And later never going home even for vacation if I could help it. Until I finally never went home at all. Yet years later in New York when my stepfather actually did wrestle me to his hotel room floor, it came as a relief, because I found I could fight him off, because I realized that I had not imagined it, that my fear of him had been real.

I see this most in situations that frighten me now. Anything that has to do with losing my equilibrium. Fear of elevators and subways. Of bicycles and roller skates. The first time a woman tried to make love to me, I pushed her away, even though no more than six months later I would look at another woman and know love for the first time. Perhaps fear is an indication of how deep something can reach inside you. Of where you are truly vulnerable.

But at that moment in Berkeley something had just begun. I thought to myself that night in early September, sitting alone in my room, staring at a small spot of blood on an empty cot where minutes before two bodies had lain, "I am here."

"Finally, I have arrived."

THE MUSICIAN & THE POET

History has a human face. Just as there are certain smells, pictures, words that evoke the memory of a particular era or locale, there are individuals who do the same. While it is true every decade is populated with people important to you, there are always two or three who define the period and your place in it, who bring it to life.

For me, during the years at Berkeley, those people were Diane Wakoski and La Monte Young.

On the cover of the Winter 1960 *Occident,* the University of California literary magazine edited that year by Diane, is a portrait she took of La Monte sitting on—or, it might appear to the casual viewer, sitting in—a rock. The photo, a snapshot really, is blurred from being enlarged and in it La Monte appears folded like a nesting bird or a brooding condor, an image not of the late Fifties or early Sixties but timeless, defined by wind and tide rather than by social convention. La Monte is clean shaven. His features seem to sink into his face in much the same way he sinks into the boulders. His lips thin, determined, he looks carved from stone himself, but not hard, inhuman. To the contrary, his hunched form makes the rocks take on a softer, living aspect, as if they had grown up purposely to support him. It is only when you look closely at his face you realize how young he is. His tight black velvet pants and pointed shoes—covered in this photo by a baggy jacket—are outlandish for the period. Although slight in build, he is wiry, there is nothing fragile about him. La Monte carries his childhood as a street-smart kid as a tangible presence, neatly, with the subtle, almost whimsical air of a pirate, yet with a hidden toughness. You could easily imagine a switchblade concealed neatly beneath his almost Shakespearean garb.

La Monte knew more about music then anyone I had ever

met, than I ever imagined it was possible to know. I think that music has always been my first love. From the time I can remember I have loved sounds, loved to beat them out with my fingers, feet, my head bobbing rhythmically to whatever cadence hung in the air. People used to laugh at me at school as I sat transfixed, unaware of my body moving and swaying, apart from any conscious effort on my part. At the age of four, I learned to play the piano, a skill that came easily. I learned to read music before I could read words. As I grew older, my talent slipped away. In one way it was too easy, in another I was pushed too hard to be an adult, to play the music that adults enjoyed, to play in front of a live audience, when my favorite audience was always one I imagined in my head. Confronting real people my fingers would inevitably slip, my mind would wander and go blank. Even today, music is still the thing I turn to when I need comfort the most, before art, literature, even the poetry that I have grown to love so much.

Because of La Monte our apartment was filled with music, but not of a kind familiar to me. With the exception of Bartok's Violin Concerto, which was a favorite of mine even as a Fifties high school student, with its odd twists and turns opening the conventional world into something strange and mysterious, I had never heard anything resembling the sounds that now filled our ears and doorways.

One evening the quiet of our home was shattered by the discordant sounds of *Gesang der Jünglinge I*, an electronic composition by Karlheinz Stockhausen. La Monte played the recording over and over until I realized I had only two choices—to come to terms with these strange new sounds or to pack up and leave. The next day after Diane and La Monte left for class, I took the recording and, sitting alone in my room, smoked the one precious joint I had hidden under a stack of textbooks, and played it until I began to hear past my preconceptions, until what was cacophony became music.

I performed in three of La Monte's concerts that I

La Monte Young, Stinson Beach, California, ca. 1959-60. *Occident*
magazine cover (University of California at Berkeley undergraduate
literary magazine)
Photo: Diane Wakoski. Copyright © Diane Wakoski 1990

remember: An opera he composed for the new Berkeley multi-million dollar auditorium in which I fried eggs in an electric frying pan my parents had sent me, as our musician friend Phyllis Jones rocked a bunch of celery while softly crooning a lullaby—a performance that had the audience roaring its disapproval. We performed at Stanford University with the same result. At UCLA we performed a piece by John Cage that consisted of coordinating a stack of instructional cards with a stop-watch to signal when to turn a radio on and off—theoretically mixing artistic intent with chance. Within sixty seconds, I was totally lost. Looking around frantically at the other performers, I had a suspicion they were too. So I kept flipping my cards, glancing at my watch, turning my radio on and off, now completely at random, but with the air of someone who was assiduously following instructions. In retrospect, I'm not sure it mattered.

I think if there was one thing that attracted me to La Monte and Diane, it was their quality of serious play, of studied imagination. Perhaps everyone has a favorite fantasy, one that is brought over from childhood, constructed of bits and pieces of storybooks and dream, a place where the real world of conflict and confusion, harsh recrimination from behind closed doors, financial worries, the sounds and catastrophe of the adult world can be closed out. The imagined world is not free from danger, but it is a danger that somehow always comes out right in the end, when after many trials you prove yourself up to the appointed task—the world of the imagination ironically more rational than the mundane world of everyday life and school and friends who never quite understand where you are, hidden as you are, deep inside yourself.

Stepping into Diane and La Monte's apartment on Telegraph Avenue, which was later also to become mine, I stepped into that other world, a world that opened up into the magic land I had dreamed of all through my childhood. At first I didn't see the cruelty possible behind its doors, the menace in its magic. Although both did exist, abundantly, it was still qualitatively different from the world of make-believe I had grown up in—the Hollywood of fake facades, false fronts, buildings that were only shells, built purposely to deceive.

At the center of this scenario was Diane. She was everything I, at nineteen, idolized, wanted to be—or at the very least to be near. For this reason she is harder for me to describe than La Monte. I don't think I have ever seen anyone physically embody opposites in the way Diane did. With shoulder-length blond, almost white, straight hair, which she often wore drawn back tightly into a bun, and round thin-rimmed glasses, from the neck up she gave the studied appearance of a prudish schoolmarm, a perfect counterpoint to the meticulously bohemian context she inhabited—one guaranteed to set her apart. Nevertheless, she often wore La Monte's jacket, and her clothing in general subtlety contradicted the stern face she sometimes put on, hiding another gentler, quite sensual persona.

Diane defined the word "poet" to me. Because of her in-ordinate talent and prodigious output, she was acknowledged as the opinionated matriarch of the Berkeley/San Francisco poetry scene even at her young age. How I envied her certainty, her conviction, how she could deliver an opinion as an ultimatum, words clenched tight around ideas, daring anyone to pull them away. She often spoke and wrote of herself with an anger and self-deprecation balanced simultaneously with sly humor and an enormous egotism that negated her words at the same time she spoke them.

There was a quality of age about Diane as if somehow she was born with a secret knowledge of the interior workings of the orange groves she called her home. She never spoke about those beginnings except in her poems—the absent father, the shadow of a mother who was never mentioned, never described—her father always standing as a metaphor of loss, an ideal to be reached for, as I reached toward her, as we follow our illusions (delusions?) until we finally, lucky or unlucky, become what we were always striving to be.

Don't expect to find "truth" here, "objectivity"—that delinquent twentieth-century fable. Older now by more than forty years, I can only try for the moment to erase more recent memories to construct a pristine view of those first encounters.

But maybe I'm mistaken after all. Maybe this is the observation of the woman I now am and not that young girl who through innocence (read: lack of experience, therefore expectation) saw quite clearly the people who surrounded her, with the necessary assistance of a naïveté that could accept and love wholeheartedly, without question or hope of recompense. Who could truly embrace what is, with all its attendant confusion and pain.

HUAC

Endless rows of men. Short. Squat. Helmets cover their foreheads. Looking like bull-dogs, they could be cartoon caricatures, but there is nothing humorous about them. The San Francisco Tactical Police Force. The riot squad. Hundreds of men flanked on each side by a phalanx of horse patrols. In each pair of clenched hands, a club held taut across their bodies, they scarcely seem to breathe.

I am in front of the courthouse in San Francisco. It is May, 1960, the day after what would later be referred to as *The House Un-American Activities Committee Police Riots.* Many people in 1960, myself included, didn't realize HUAC was still in existence until it was announced they would be holding hearings in San Francisco. I had seen the Army-McCarthy Hearings on TV in 1954 and had taken it for granted that after McCarthy was discredited by Joseph Welsh the committee had eventually disbanded.

"Don't move too fast!"

"Don't threaten them!"

Whatever you do, don't set them in motion. Walk slowly, slowly, around and around and around in an oval in front of the courthouse steps, where the day before peaceful demonstrators had been washed down the long flights of stone steps—fire hoses turned on them full blast. Walk, staring straight ahead, the heat searing under that brilliant San Francisco sun. Walk, not knowing how long the path would be, how many years it would stretch across. How many states, how many countries it would encompass. Beginning on this day in San Francisco, California, in the glare of the noonday sun.

I wasn't really afraid. I had never been to a demonstration before, had never seen demonstrators dragged through the streets, beaten bloody, senseless, to the ground. I couldn't, even in my wildest imagination, see police racing toward demonstrators, see the utter chaos that produces. Running from no one, from everyone. The crowd around you as much a danger as the clubs. Everyone trying to get away. Police appearing from nowhere, then vanishing back into the crowd. That experience would come later, in the late Sixties, in front of another courthouse, the snow piled high around us, mid-winter New York so different from that blistering day in San Francisco when everything stretched endlessly in one direction—ahead.

Now I only saw what seemed an infinite amount of force threatening to strike. The clubs more alive, more mobile than the men. But that day it was an abstraction, a curiosity. What I saw in front of me, to each side, was so outside anything I had ever experienced it lacked all sense of tangible reality. Fear is built on the lived consequences of an action, not on some intellectual notion, and for the moment a stand-off had been achieved, the city not prepared then, as they would be later, to take on more than 2500 students, not sure yet what that might mean.

Writing about past events is at best a precarious venture, much like looking at an old photo album, at yourself years younger, at people you loved, who loved you and are gone. Sometimes the only thing you can remember about the past is an old snapshot, losing color, becoming vaguely tinted as if half of it were already in another world.

Justice as a concept is equally hard to define. For some it means a redress of wrongs. For others, like the ancient Egyptians, justice means *Ma'at*, harmony, balance—not only the balance between good and evil deeds judged at the time of death, it is also the balance that orders the universe, keeps the planets in orbit, protects us against chaos, controls the moments of time. In practice, justice is not a point to be argued, the circumstances all too clear.

In 1959/1960 the artists and political people in Berkeley

lived separate lives for the most part, but went to some of the same parties, hung out at the same bars, occasionally slept with each other and lined up together against the "frat crowd." And when demonstrators were washed down the steps of the San Francisco courthouse, including our friends Donna Worth and her husband Carl, the artists from New York who lived down the hall, an emergency meeting of Berkeley students was called, and along with hundreds of other students, Diane and La Monte and I were there.

As I remember it, the room was large and bare, students everywhere, some sitting on chairs, the floor, some leaning against the walls. First one student spoke and then another. The sounds overlapping like chords, it was hard to tell when one speech ended and the next began. But there was little discord. There was no debate about the need for a response to the police brutality; there was no debate about the course of action we should take.

This was 1960 and we were guided by the precepts of the Civil Rights Movement and the need to attract as large a crowd as possible. There was no notion of going beyond peaceful picketing, a demonstration of our support for the students who had been brutalized. We were anxious to show that the students who had protested that day did not stand alone in their opposition to the House UnAmerican Activities Committee.

This was the first time I had ever been involved in a meeting with so many people working together collectively— most of whom had never met before that night. It was hard for me to concentrate on what any individual was saying, I was so overwhelmed by the sheer number of people, their enthusiasm and commitment.

Even more compelling than the actions we were planning was the camaraderie. It went beyond anything I had ever thought possible, coming, as I did, from a world of secrecy and competition.

The images of that night and the day that followed are disjointed, disconnected in memory, just as they were disjointed, disconnected then, having no context in which to frame them, no history lived or read that would help them make any sense—the police, the hundreds of demonstrators, Diane and La Monte and I, a shared orange soda, the hours of endless marching, the heat of the sun.

I was barely conscious of the courthouse building we circled in front of, seeing only the demonstrators before and behind me, what seemed like endless lines of horses and police—all against a background that appeared to extend endlessly into the horizon. Although the courthouse must have been set in among many more buildings, all I could see was that one building outlined against the sky, nothing around it but people and space. If there were onlookers I don't remember them, just the flat surfaces of concrete, the riot squad, the police on horseback arranged in three perfect squares, north, east, west—the fourth side, the courthouse—the demonstrators marching in the area where the police and building met.

At times I felt like I was looking at the scene from a suspended vantage point, our individual figures, even the individual figures of the police, looking so small in the context of the hundreds, perhaps thousands of people occupying the same space.

I doubt that is exactly how it looked, but that is how it played itself out in my mind. I didn't remember even then how we got to the courthouse or how we finally got back home. It was as if we had been positioned in that place by some alien force with no center of gravity except our own momentum to hold us in place.

It was after that incident that I first began to lead my "double life," my deception ranging from ideas to the way I dressed. When it came time to go home, I carefully filled my suitcases with "normal" clothes, leaving my sandals and black skirt and sweater and soiled raincoat neatly folded in a dresser drawer.

During spring break I realized just how important my artifice was for my survival.

The *Los Angeles Examiner*, an extremely conservative newspaper, ran a series of articles accusing the demonstrators at the HUAC hearings of being Communist dupes, if not outright Communists themselves.

One morning I came down to breakfast to find my stepfather sitting at the breakfast table reading a headline that went something like *Reds Instigate Berkeley Riot*. Slamming the paper down on the table and looking me full in the face, he blurted out angrily: "You're not involved in any of this are you?"

"No," I lied. "Why?"

"Good. Because if I thought you were, even though you're my daughter, I would be the first one to turn you in to the FBI."

I believed him.

I never spoke to my parents about anything that was important to me again.

LOVE & OTHER CRISES

With all its magic, Berkeley was not a particularly sweet time. Its colors were bold, vivid, a patina drawn in passion and surprise. In one corner of my bedroom ceiling where the paint was peeling, I could see the incandescent blue some enterprising soul had painted years before. It looked like a grotesque scar, fluorescent in feeling and hue. Lying on my bed staring up at it, I felt like I was skidding on the surface of an old 78 RPM phonograph record, spinning faster and faster inexorably toward the center.

I had never really thought much about love or romance. As an adolescent, I was more concerned with day-to-day details—keeping my summer job, passing my French class, surviving family scenes. By my junior year, I had a steady boyfriend, whom I liked well enough but with whom I was not particularly involved emotionally. College was much the same except, instead of one, there were many men.

When love did happen it was sudden, unexpected, sure. It was a moment I knew instantly would remain recorded in my memory to the last detail: the texture of the air, stale, spiced with the smells drifting up from the grocery store downstairs; my hands slightly sticky, sweating from the sometimes oppressive Berkeley heat; the weight of the books I was carrying; the shock as emotional attachment (the longing to be with one particular person, the feeling of loss when they were gone) collided with sexual attraction and the two blurred and meshed.

Even now how hard it is for me to write these words, how hard it is to pretend that although more than forty years separate me from the young woman I once was, I can successfully distance myself from her, the distress she felt, the longing that haunts me still.

It was an ordinary day, nothing out of the usual: hot, sunny, but dull. A flat day. I was tired and looked forward to getting home to dinner and a nap. At first when I entered the rooms I shared with Diane and La Monte, it was so quiet I thought no one was home. The door was unlocked, a signal it was okay for me to come through the living room door. I could also get to my room through the kitchen, which ensured Diane and La Monte privacy when they needed it, since the living room also served as their bedroom. It was an access I only used when the living room door was locked since it entailed climbing out the kitchen window onto a landing that connected our building with the roof next door and walking along outside the living room and climbing back through my window. It was an easy procedure, unless it happened to be raining, but it was much more convenient just to walk through Diane and La Monte's room when that was possible—which was most of the time.

Only a few months before that fateful afternoon, Marsha, a close friend, had tried to make love to me. It was a Friday night, and I had stayed at her apartment because we had been at a party and it was late and I didn't want to make the long trip home. She had only one bed, so we shared it. I didn't think anything of sleeping in the same bed with her. After all, she was another woman. Even though Marsha was gentle and tentative and backed off immediately when I pulled away, her advances terrified me. Despite her pleas to lie down and sleep, nothing more would happen, I spent the rest of the night sitting on the edge of the bed, shaken, smoking one cigarette after another.

And now, I stood, no more than six months later, watching Diane lying quietly on the sofa with John, a friend, in her arms, comforting him. They were both dressed. There was nothing sexual in their embrace—John was gay. But as I looked at her holding him, the tenderness in her arms, the way she stroked his face, she looked so beautiful to me all I wanted was to be that young boy, held by her. I wanted to reach out to her and touch her and hold her. I wanted her to make love to me with that special tenderness, even though I had no idea what our making love would entail.

I had never felt that way before about Diane, not during the dozens of times I had seen her in bed with La Monte, the dozens of times I had seen her in the apartment or at school. And now I stood, dumb, at six o'clock in the evening, the sun at least an hour from setting, while Diane turned and, smiling at me, told me what had happened to John and asked me how my day had gone, just like she might have done any other day, in any other circumstance. It wasn't a moment that arrived accompanied by a dramatic drum roll, a symphony in the background or even an anemic hum. Nothing was transformed. Nothing acknowledged that anything special had taken place.

I never spoke of my feelings to Diane. Never in all the time we were friends, even though the strength of that love remained intact through many years, through many actualized relationships with both women and men.

Ironically, in 1960, in the Berkeley I lived in, with all its bohemian attitudes and sexual and political experimentation, there was no way to articulate to anyone the way I felt, no way to understand it myself, to visualize in concrete terms what it meant, much less to act it out. The numerous sexual encounters I had by then with men held no clue about how to behave in this strange new situation.

So, at the age of twenty, I fell in love for the first time. It was almost a decade before the activism of the "second wave" of the women's movement and the gay liberation movement. There was no support system, no literature, not even a hint of what I was supposed to feel, or more importantly, do with my new discovery. I didn't think of myself as being "gay" or even "bisexual." I was in love with Diane and could not see beyond her to anyone else, male *or* female.

Later, when I began to realize my attraction to women, I was no more able to fit into the Fifties and early Sixties gay world with its traditional roles than I had found myself able to fit into the conventional "straight" world. The more hip "queer world" of the poets, which was almost exclusively male, was also out of reach.

Consequently, I waded at random through most of the confusions and psychological conundrums available to a person with little experience and almost unlimited opportunity. Until finally, looking one morning in the mirror, I wondered just who it was I saw staring back at me, so little did I feel at that point that I even fit into the human race. Not in dress, not in attitude, not in intellectual interests, not in my art, my poetry, and certainly not in my recognition of myself as a woman.

Nowhere did I recognize anything familiar, anything I could name, or, more important, touch.

The pain I felt that night when I finally closed myself in my room, closed in upon myself in my room, was exactly as I remembered my first terrible feeling of homesickness as a five-year-old child—the unnamed physical sensation that settled somewhere in my chest, the heaviness that kept me from food, that rendered me sleepless.

While Diane and La Monte remained in Berkeley, I continued sleeping with men. Outwardly I acted exactly the same as I had before. Inwardly, everything had changed.

In 1960, when Diane and La Monte moved first to San Francisco and then to New York, the apartment was mine, and I shared it first with one and then a half-dozen other students. One night it was so crowded with sleeping bodies when I came home—three, even four to a bed—I had to go to Donna and Carl's apartment to sleep. My apartment had become a sanctuary from the grown-up world, a kind of pre-adolescent space. It was an unaffected innocence; it was understood implicitly that while we were all together this was a space free of sex, alcohol (except for a glass of wine or beer) and drugs. The issue never really came up. A package of crayons and a stack of paper always lay by the kitchen door, and I often came home in the evening from work or school to see a friend or even a stranger sitting at the kitchen table coloring, or pasting her or his new artwork on the wall. One day I returned home to a drawing of a red horse dangling from the ceiling, all the spaces in our impromptu gallery being filled.

I was never afraid. These were my friends, even the ones I didn't know. They protected me. My door was always unlocked. If someone needed food, they could enter and eat. They always did something in return, like one unknown friend who took the last of our cheese and for payment mopped the floor.

But like everything else, our sanctuary was temporary. In that gubernatorial election year, a great wave of political reaction had already begun. One night over four hundred people in San Francisco, particularly in the booming North Beach area, the home of jazz and poetry, were arrested on drug charges. The next day all but seven were released, but the message was clear. People flooded into Berkeley. Among them was Larry, a streetwise painter who introduced me to his friend Ward, an African American honor student in psychology with a fancy Harley Davidson motorcycle and a very sweet temperament, who took up residence in my apartment and became a prime mover in our little commune.

One night, several weeks after Ward moved in, I came home to find a gang of white teenagers from Oakland in front of our apartment building. Angered by rumors that blacks were living there with white students, they were lined up in two rows, each of them holding a thick bicycle chain, screaming racial epithets and rage. Fearful that something had happened to Ward or one of our friends, I pushed past them, throwing open the door to our apartment complex.

Standing on the stairs that led up to our floor, Ward and

several of his friends stood guard. As soon as he saw me, he rushed down the stairs and hurried me into the apartment, telling me to lock the door until he was sure it was safe—which I refused to do, partly from bravado, mostly from ignorance. Ward was much more aware than I was of the consequences of what was taking place. To me, it all seemed unreal, something that happened in movies or on the news reports on TV, about foreign countries, the South, certainly not Berkeley, not our hip world that pretended away boundaries and difference.

Standing in that stairwell, looking at the faces on the street full of hatred, the faces of my friends on the stairs, anxious, prepared for anything—I was filled with dread. This was not fantasy or fiction and it was not unique. It was a scene that had been repeated before and would most likely be repeated again. The dread turned to terror, but it was too late to retreat. I had chosen out of ignorance to make a stand, now out of knowledge I had to remain in place. The more frightened I became, the more my throat seemed to constrict until I felt I could hardly force air into my lungs, so I tried to focus on my breathing. Slowly inhaling, slowly exhaling. Trying to look calm, confident. Trying not to show how I really felt.

Fortunately, word about what was going down had gotten around and groups of students and supporters began gathering until finally, after what seemed like hours, the gang dispersed, dissolving almost in seconds from the street. There was not a policemen to be seen.

That night was my first lesson about divisions and what living them means. Soon after, Ward left the apartment to move in with his girlfriend, but we still went out together often. I loved riding on the back of his motorcycle, particularly when we rode down by the water or on the long winding roads that wove through the Berkeley hills. Once we rode all the way to Tilden Park. Surrounded by trees and dusk, it was easy to pretend I was in another world, one without streets and windows and grades and parents and endless anxiety and secrets and deception.

One night Ward and I were walking down a quiet Berkeley street. We had just come from the movies and were trying to decide whether to go home or stop for something to eat when two patrolmen stopped us demanding we roll up our sleeves and show them our arms. At first I had no idea what they were talking about; then I realized they were checking us for needle marks. Either they couldn't imagine that a white woman would be out on the street late at night with a black man for any other reason or it was quite simply a warning—this was what we could expect if we continued to be together, even as friends.

My love for Diane opened me in a way I had never thought possible. Being with Ward threw me up against racism in a way I had never experienced in the shelter of my family's admonitions. Of the many lessons I learned at Berkeley during those years, those two were easily the most profound, teaching me, as they did, what I might expect in retaliation from a world whose values I was growing more and more to reject.

BARRY & MARIE

The summer Diane and La Monte left, I acquired two new neighbors. Barry was a graduate student in sociology who had returned to the University after several years of trying unsuccessfully to make a living doing odd jobs. He seemed pleasant enough whenever I saw him alone, which was seldom, but next to his diminutive wife he appeared gross and loud. She was always huddled so close to him she seemed more like an appendage than a human partner. Marie, even apart from Barry, was a strange woman. Attractive more in attitude than physical appearance, she was one of those women who age early, her face and demeanor old for her thirty-two years. But it was her voice that was compelling. It was low, almost a whisper, with a seductive quality that required you to move close to her to discover what she was saying.

Marie seemed to inhale everything into her, absorbing anyone who came within hearing distance. I was fascinated by her and quite soon could think of no one else. On any excuse, I took to visiting her in their tiny back room apartment.

By comparison, my own space was grand with its attached kitchen and two adjacent rooms. Even the single room I had occupied when I shared the space with Diane and La Monte had a huge bay window in the front that allowed light to pour in all hours of the day.

Marie was a twilight person, illumined only by the indirect rays of sunlight that filtered through the roof of the building next door, her only view of the world one small window facing a blank concrete wall. I seldom saw her outside her cramped quarters. I wondered sometimes how often she went outdoors. It was hard to avoid envisioning her sneaking out in the dead of night, wrapped in some dark disguise that would allow her to blend into the buildings so wherever she passed, she could pass unseen.

It was a rainy August afternoon when Marie and I first kissed. From the time I woke up that morning, I had felt something tenuous about the day. Although the summers could be cold in Berkeley, it seldom rained. The constant sound of drops pelting the window panes was friendly, comforting, but foreign. The building for once seemed deserted. The various occupants—mostly artists, writers, and students—were either out or locked into their diverse preoccupations.

Toward the middle of the afternoon, I heard Barry and Marie's door slam and Barry's heavy step. He often went out alone for hours at a time, so this seemed a perfect opportunity to pay Marie a visit. I didn't have anything special in mind. I was fascinated by Marie, but had no illusion about being with her sexually, although it was obviously sex—even if I didn't know it then—that drew me to her.

Consequently, I didn't expect this day to be out of the ordinary. I expected it to consist of an hour or two of small talk, maybe some gossip about the other roomers in the building. Marie fancied herself a raconteur and artist, although she rarely talked or painted. Oddly enough, with all her aged demeanor, there was something childlike about her. The one time we had gone out together, we had spent the entire afternoon on one of the wide green lawns that studded the university, squatting on the grass like two kindergarten students, chattering about nothing, drawing trees and flowers and caricatures of the expressions on the faces of people who passed.

But it was not that lovely afternoon that made me think, even then, of Marie as childlike. It was a way she had of making a statement and then hiding behind her hand, giggling as if she had just said the silliest thing imaginable. With all that she reeked sexuality. It was an unbeatable combination.

But this afternoon was different. Marie started the conversation by saying that Barry had a project due the following week and would be at the library the entire afternoon. He might not even be back for dinner. This, in and of itself, was unusual, since she rarely mentioned Barry at all when we were together. We talked for a while, laughed a bit. I sat at the small wooden table that doubled as their eating space and work table nervously building imaginary houses with a small pile of emptied sugar wrappers. Barry had painted the table crimson. It was the only real color in the room and stood out like a festering wound against the pale gray skin of the walls.

In the middle of a sentence, Marie patted the space next to her on the bed where she was seated. There was only enough space in her room for one chair, so the bed served, as it did in all our rooms, as a daytime sofa. She coughed a little, as if it were too much effort to speak loud enough for me to hear—which was absurd, since I was no more than three or four feet away, but I happily played along and sat down beside her.

The next thing I knew she reached over and gingerly touching the side of my neck, as if to test the waters, kissed me full on the mouth.

My reaction was quite different from what it had been months before with Marsha. Marie and I kissed for what seemed like hours. I felt dizzy with the sensation of being with her, astonished by it. I never wanted it to end.

But finally Marie whispered, "You'll have to leave. It's getting late and I have to fix dinner before Barry comes home. But we'll see each other again soon, very soon. I promise…very soon…."

Two days later I visited Marie again. We immediately took up where we had left off. I didn't feel the same kind of credulous surprise, but it felt good—and right. Suddenly Marie stopped and pushing me away, scurried over to the two-burner hot plate that served as her stove. Without a word, she took her only pot and filling it with water, set it to boil. There was something in the deliberateness with which she was moving, the silence in the room, that was ominous. Staring at the water beginning to boil, it was hard for me to fend off a premonition of myself dancing among the steaming bubbles.

In the midst of sorting through her collection of herbal tea bags, Marie turned toward me and in that low breathy whisper of hers, now spiced with a sardonic undertone, she murmured softly, savoring each word: "Drinking tea. Isn't that what lesbians do after they make love?"

She then launched, in a voice filled with more passion— and volume—than I had ever heard, into a tirade about how wonderful sex with her husband was. How wonderful it was to have a "real man" make love to you, to be held in the strong arms of a man. How she could hardly wait until Barry came home at night. How everything paled by comparison.

I didn't wait for the tea to be poured. I stuttered some excuse about having to get back to work and left.

I never visited Marie's room again.

Years later, Marie came to New York and we had lunch together. I had no intention of mentioning what had happened between us, but in the middle of our reminiscences about Berkeley, she broke in with an apology, explaining she didn't know why she had treated me so badly when she genuinely liked me, adding that she and Barry had actually been in the middle of getting a divorce at the time—which was why he had been gone so often. Besides, all the things she had told me about him making love to her were a lie, she really hated sleeping with him.

I nodded and shrugged it off. By that time I was getting used to doing deliberately what I had done that day so long ago instinctively—concealing what those few hours with her had meant to me, what it had meant to me to be called a lesbian (a word that terrified me then), what it had meant to be told by her how much better it was to be held by a man at the very moment it seemed like finally my life was opening up, that finally, for me, there was a chance.

FANTASY & MORNING GLORY SEEDS

In February, Sylvia Gold moved into the little room formerly occupied by Max and his wife. The room had a separate entrance to the hall, but it was considered part of my space so it was up to me to find a tenant.

The morning Sylvia arrived, she found both me and the apartment in a state of disarray. We had had a party the night before that was to become the talk of Berkeley for years to come. It had started out as a small birthday party for Larry. I had invited no more than fourteen or fifteen people, but somehow the word had gotten around San Francisco and before the night was out over two hundred people crowded into my apartment, filling it, then all the rooms on our floor, and finally the floor above us—everyone in the building at this point joining in. Even the roof outside the kitchen window that had served as my private entranceway the year before was filled with laughing, dancing people. On one corner of the roof two sailors from San Francisco spent the night necking with each other, while in the middle of the living room, a young Persian electrical engineering student with whom I had slept a couple of times, knelt, hands clasped, praying loudly for my soul. Every half hour or so he would come over to me, usually when I was dancing or drinking, pull sadly at my sleeve, and then, rebuffed, return to the same spot on the floor, and begin praying again.

The party went on past dawn until I was left alone with Ward and Larry, an enormous hangover, and an empty apartment. Like a swarm of locusts, my uninvited guests had departed taking most of my apartment as souvenirs. I can only imagine that was their motivation since I had nothing of any real value. Even the place mats on the kitchen table and two small cheap throw rugs that had proudly decorated my living room floor were gone. I sat drunkenly bemoaning the betrayal I had suffered, until I was persuaded to take a cold shower and finally, clothed in an old, but flamboyant blue velour robe, fell asleep.

Not more than two hours later there was a loud knock at the door and into this chaos Sylvia arrived. I took one look at her and decided she was definitely not the right person for my empty space. She was neatly dressed in a conservative reddish-brown skirt, low heels, and an all-to-obviously freshly ironed white shirt and was carrying a large tan suitcase. To my eyes, she fairly radiated bourgeois respectability and health, and it didn't help my opinion of her to learn she had just graduated from Barnard College. In my ignorance, all I had to hear was that Barnard was a women's college in the East and I automatically figured it for one of those fancy women's finishing schools.

The reality was that Sylvia was from a working class Jewish family from Brooklyn and was almost certainly more down-to-earth than I was.

I did everything I could to discourage her from taking the room, acting as stupid as possible, lurching around the room exaggerating my headache, the building's noise, the long wait for the shared bathroom in the hall, the impossible logistics of sharing the kitchen, but all to no avail. She wanted the space, and she got it.

Within the year, Sylvia and I would be lovers.

About a month after Sylvia arrived, I had a miscarriage. In those days the specter of pregnancy hung over every heterosexual relationship. Abortion was illegal, and even in my circles where all kinds of information freely circulated, it was difficult, and always extremely expensive to find a doctor to perform the operation safely. Those who legislated against abortion also made it almost impossible for women to get adequate birth control. A man could buy a condom, but to get a diaphragm, a woman had to produce a marriage certificate. Even years later Bil Baird, the puppeteer, was arrested in Massachusetts for publicly advocating and displaying birth control devices.

I usually was very careful. It was well before the advent of AIDS, but in addition to the fear of pregnancy, there were other sexually transmitted diseases that, if ultimately curable, were highly dangerous if not properly treated. The problem was when you drink you take risks. And although I didn't drink often, I did like to party.

On this particular occasion my period was almost a month late. I wasn't overly concerned—with my hectic lifestyle, my period was often irregular. I decided, as a break from my heavy work schedule, to try out a new "legal" high that was floating around. The penalties for being found with even a little marijuana were severe, so there was a lot of experimenting with drugs that were not officially illegal.

The chemistry department at Berkeley was a constant source of creative energy.

This was before LSD was widely available, but every month or so another recipe for a hallucinogen would make the rounds. First, there was a recipe for a concoction of whole nutmeg baked with milk for four hours and then crushed and eaten by the tablespoon, which was supposed to have been told to some anonymous student by a prisoner as a secret way the prison population got high. After spending days finding a place to get whole nutmeg and hours cooking the mixture, I finally got down a half teaspoon and decided it wasn't worth it.

That was followed by detailed instructions on how to cut slots out of a piece of cardboard which was then made into a cone and placed on a turntable with a light bulb suspended through it to make it into a strobe. You were then instructed to sit in front of it, eyes closed, until colors started dancing through your brain. It gave me a headache.

They took morning glory seeds off the market before I could get to them.

This particular week the news was that Romular, an over-the-counter cough suppressant in pill form, would give you an extraordinary high. I called Ward and we circled Berkeley and then Oakland until we finally found a drugstore that still had some of the pills left in stock—as soon as the manufacturers realized why there was such a run on their product it was taken off most drugstore shelves. The catch was you had to overdose on thirty pills or more to get any effect. I started out with fifteen, and then took another fifteen an hour later. The drug did work. It wasn't a hallucinogen, but had the strange effect of distorting distance so that you couldn't judge how far away or how near you were to an object. It was like turning off the third dimension in your brain. It was an intellectual, rather than a visual or auditory sensation.

I wasn't afraid of taking so much of the medication since a number of people I knew had taken it with no ill effect, but about twenty minutes after I swallowed the second batch of pills I was hit with a wave of nausea. The drug magnified the sensation intolerably. I ran into the bathroom and was wracked with dry heaves, almost passing out several times. I was sure I was dying.

I pleaded with Ward to take me to the hospital, but he cautioned me to wait. I didn't appear to be that sick, and he knew the effect a drug can have on magnifying anxiety. His reassurance made me feel better, and I was finally beginning to settle down when I was seized by abdominal cramping and blood started pouring out of me. It didn't last long, but it was obvious my period had started. It was also obvious something more than my period had happened.

After that, the partying and the promiscuity stopped.

Enough was enough.

Around that time, a treasure came into my possession. In those days, along with the ban on abortion and the difficulty in obtaining adequate birth control, strict censorship was imposed on all written and broadcast material of everything except, supposedly, the news media. Only a few years before there had been an attempt to censor the last chapter of James Joyce's *Ulysses*. Even the edition of *Gulliver's Travels* sold in the United States was expurgated and Allen Ginsberg's poem *Howl*—and Allen Ginsberg—became famous when the post office tried to make it illegal to send it through the mail and an important court case ensued. Many authors, including D. H. Lawrence, William Burroughs, and Henry Miller, were proscribed, and their books were printed and available only outside the United States.

I had given a friend who was going to Mexico forty dollars—more than a week's pay—to purchase two books, and she had just returned with Henry Miller's *Tropic of Cancer* and William Burrough's *The Naked Lunch*.

It would be the late Sixties before the censorship laws were finally overturned.

I often felt as if I drifted through those years in a kind of haze, seeing things happening around me, participating, but at a distance, until one night I was sitting hunched over a piano in an extraordinary house in the Berkeley Hills designed by an eccentric who had built a canal through the middle of the living room floor, complete with running water and multi-colored goldfish, listening to a record of Lotta Lenya singing the theater songs of Kurt Weill in German when I was overcome by a tangible awareness of the space I was in, the city, my place in it.

In the middle of a strange room, surrounded by people I hardly knew, a language I couldn't understand, I finally felt centered, completely at home.

But soon it would be time for me to leave. Stage one of my journey was almost over. Diane had written me from New York, and I knew that was where I would go, the next place where the world that was now a part of me would take me.

LETTING GO

*"I hate you and as long as I'm alive I'll fight you." Hands shaking,
my body exists only as a fist. "I hate you and as long as I hate you I can live."
The walls move. The face smiles. The voices disappear. The chair, large,
slides over me. My hands become old, wrinkled. The room is squares
and cubes, and triangles. The colors, blinding, form into patterns.
The rocking begins. Lines fall apart, curve, ropes, twisting, unbearable.*

The two tiny blue pills of psilocybin I had taken were slow to
work. By the time I began to feel anything, it was getting
dark. I was dozing in that semiconscious state between
sleeping and waking, when my attention was caught by a
strange weaving light just beyond my line of vision. It was
coming from the door that led to the hallway. The crack of
light at the bottom of the door and the crack of light at the
top were beginning to undulate, to slowly come together, join,
and then slip apart.

The sight fascinated me. It was hypnotic. I couldn't move
my eyes away from the outline of the door, which by then
had begun to alternately shrink and grow in size. Color began
to gain in intensity, the green of the chair next to me
becoming so deep I felt I could put my hand through the
center of it, pull the now liquid color out of it and stretch and
fold it against me. Each maroon and purple candle in the
milk-white clay wine bottles that circled the molding on the
walls, the shelves enclosed in a pine wood bookshelf fronted
by faded yellow glass, the multicolored covers of my books—
all were coming alive with color, were beginning to separate
out from their component parts and move in increasingly
complex patterns until I was forced to shut my eyes, shut out
the confusion of my senses, smell and sound and color
blossoming into a life of their own.

Opening my eyes again to the strangeness wildly gyrating
around me, I was startled by the image of my own face in the
mirror, features I barely recognized as mine, growing as they
were, beckoning to me as if I were a person apart from them,

my left eye deepening into color until it became a brilliant turquoise, my other eye fading entirely away, until that single huge eye swallowed first my face, then my entire body, as I saw myself reflected in my now giant pupil.

I was torn between curiosity and longing, excitement and sadness—the beauty and intensity of the movement and color around me colliding with the sharp sensations of loneliness and injury flowing out of me in ever-widening waves of emotion. I had asked a friend to stay with me through the night—I had never taken a hallucinogen before—but after agreeing, she had made some excuse and left, leaving me alone and restless, frightened and abandoned, the very feelings I had consciously tried to avoid.

My mouth grimaced, the muscles of my cheeks, my lips out of control, but still there was no sound. No cry issued from my mouth, just a maelstrom of visual images without voice, projected into that giant eyeball.

At my feet I could see the reflection of my cat playing with a new brood of kittens, the animal oblivious to the silent drama being acted out in such close proximity, and I decided to become a cat, to become oblivious too.

I began to play with two of the kittens who were climbing a small ladder that had been left by a neighbor who was painting her wall, and the kittens recognized and treated me like another cat, even though in physical appearance I still looked human. But to me everything suddenly seemed dulled. My senses were sharper, but my mind was slow, dense, and I remembered what it was to be human and was bored, and I pushed away the kitten who was trying to get my attention, pushed away the kitten now meowing his displeasure at my lack of response to his tiny paws raking at my hand.

All I wanted to do was cut away the images that flooded around me, and I took a knife and began cutting at my hand without noticing it, because there was no blood and no pain. I only realized what I had done days later, when I noticed, almost by accident, the lace work of almost invisible scratches across both my palms.

As the aching inside me became more solid, more intense, slowly, and then with more determination, I began to dissolve the room into elemental forms and shapes, into lines and circles—determined to stop the pain, if necessary to drive myself mad.

And then, as I had almost succeeded, when nothing remained but lines and abstract patterns weaving through the air, I pictured myself lying on my bed, the paisley sheet twisted in my hands, words now streaming out of my mouth, whimpering and talking and crying, above my head a poster of Sviatoslav Richter hunched over a piano, four tiny kittens on the floor.

And I laughed.

I saw myself trying to drive myself mad. I saw myself, words flowing endlessly, senselessly from my mouth, and it seemed so absurd that I laughed.

And the movement stopped.

The room once again became a room.

I sat upright on the bed, laughing quietly now. Feeling light, as if something had been lifted from me, something I had carried for too long. An anger I had never recognized. A hatred I had never acknowledged, never allowed myself to feel.

When I left home, all I'd thought about was what lay ahead, the only feeling I remembered was one of relief. I never understood until that night the years that lay hidden beneath my escape.

The darkness in the room steadily gave way to the light that precedes dawn. I threw on my coat and walked out into the deserted streets, the visual distortions gone, the colors and sensations still intense, intact. I thought of the story of Jacob wrestling with the angel and reached into the morning—the crisis, for the moment at least, over. Stepping into the day, everything lost and gained.

LOS ANGELES 1961:
Sometime in the Forties

I could have loved you forever Mom   if you had let me
as it was I left   gave you hardly a backward glance
kept you from becoming my world

Only to find the world becoming you...

HOME

Does shame have a color? Is it a sound that haunts you, pressing constantly against another stronger determination to search for something more compassionate, more real? Is it the same texture as the sky that June morning in Berkeley as I packed my bags to return home, a slow, steady rain covering everything in mist? It always seemed to rain whenever it came time for me to move. This time the heaviness of the sky and my mood matched perfectly. I felt as if I were returning home a stranger, not sure of what I would find, how I would react.

For years I was reluctant to let anyone know where I grew up. If asked, I would reply vaguely L.A., not wanting to fall into the stereotypes that Beverly Hills implies. How ironic that my mother, growing up poor in an immigrant family, was ashamed of her background, while I, growing up in Beverly Hills, felt the same about mine. But with that reticence came its counterpart, a growing realization of how much my upbringing had taught me about the truth behind the media images American society would come more and more to embrace.

In late June, 1961, three weeks after finishing school, I arrived at my family's front door. In less than two weeks, I would leave once again, this time for New York, not to return for over fifteen years. Even if I had not been forced to leave, I would have gone anyway, drawn by Diane's letters and the lure of a future bound in fantasy and poems. There was nothing to keep me in California, and everything to entice me away.

The house I returned to that summer was one I barely remembered. Each time my stepfather's fortunes fell, we would move into a smaller house (or apartment) in a "less desirable" part of the city. It was necessary for his business

43

as an actor's agent to maintain a Beverly Hills address, possible even with a change in fortune since Beverly Hills neighborhoods, at least in those days, ranged from modest apartments to the ostentatious estates located above Sunset Boulevard. Class boundaries were clearly delineated by parallel boulevards. Between Santa Monica and Sunset Boulevards—the next most desirable location—lived the moderately (often *nouveau*) rich. Santa Monica Boulevard to Wilshire Boulevard consisted of the business district and some lower middle-class/working-class homes and apartments. The area between Wilshire and Olympic Boulevards was home to the professional upper middle class and middle class; Olympic to Pico, middle class, lower middle class, some working class. Los Angeles neighborhoods in those days were racially "restricted." A "gentleman's agreement" on the part of buyers and sellers. Beverly Hills—white. Bel-Air—no Jews allowed.

Although there were some elite shops and restaurants on Wilshire Boulevard, most commercial activity took place along Beverly Boulevard, which housed moderately priced restaurants, a deli, miscellaneous clothing and sundries stores, a bookstore, and a movie theater where I went on Saturday as a child to see cartoons and the latest chapter of Flash Gordon and once a year to be called onto the stage to eat a piece of birthday cake. There was nothing like the row of ultra expensive shops that wind off into Rodeo Drive today.

My stepfather was never wealthy enough to make it above Sunset Boulevard, but when my mother married him he was only blocks away, living in a large Spanish-style house complete with servants and pool, located a short distance from the Beverly Hills Hotel. The house I returned to in 1961, at least four removed from those days, was a much more modest, one-story ranch house, sans servants and pool, on the edge of the business district, barely sheltered from the noisy traffic of Santa Monica Boulevard by a narrow row of trees. My parents would continue to move every few years, ending their lives finally in an apartment close to Olympic Boulevard, a half-block away from the high school.

I had no qualms about leaving California. As much as I loved Berkeley, it was hard to find work, and it seemed to me too easy to wander directionless into old age. But most of all, I hated the earthquakes. I was traumatized by an earthquake when I was very young and had no desire to repeat the experience. (4 AM: All sounds from the outside go dead, and then the loud rumble of thunder, except from the earth not the sky. And then slow, steady shaking, as I lay terrified, watching cracks snake down from ceiling to floor, up from floor to ceiling.)

I had only packed a small suitcase in preparation for the flight home since I would be driving to New York from Berkeley. I might not have gone home at all, but I was still feeling poorly from a siege of mononucleosis in the fall. My doctor at home had advised treatments with gamma globulin to clear my blood. It was his opinion I had acquired the disease in the university hospital—I had been admitted there with a severe case of the flu two weeks before I came down with "mono." In those days they didn't have disposable needles in the hospitals and he said that institutional methods of sterilizing needles were inadequate for both mono and hepatitis. Since my blood count was still borderline, I needed at least a week's treatment and as much rest as possible.

As I sat in the airport waiting for my flight to be called, I couldn't help dwelling on that other great journey in my life, when I first arrived in California as a young child. All I really remember clearly of that initial four-day train trip to Los Angeles on the Super Chief was throwing up across some three thousand miles of railroad tracks. It was as if my body already knew what waited for me in my grand new house.

It was 1943. I was four years old.

From the outside our new home seemed small, not at all like what my mother had described as we bounced across the breadth of the United States, seeing cities flash past our train window. My mother had never actually seen the house, constructing it entirely from photographs and promises. 803 North Bedford Drive. A row of giant palm trees lining the street made the sidewalks feel familiar, like the boulevards in the working-class neighborhood in Miami we had left only a few days before. But our Florida home was a three-room bungalow attached to a long row of bungalows, sided by other identical rows of bungalows, indistinguishable from each other in outline, individualized by paint and pride.

This California home was set back from the street, its face partially veiled by a large tree, as if hiding from the intrusive eyes of the houses which bordered it. I couldn't see any other people, any other children, only houses separated by grass and plants and trees. In Miami there were always people sitting in the white steel lawn chairs chatting. There were always children eager to play.

But this new house *was* pretty. There were red flowers lining the well-manicured bushes adjacent to the front door, and the Spanish facade, coated with white stucco, preened in the midday sun, its graceful arches accented by a gently sloping red tile roof. Everything looked freshly scrubbed— the neatly trimmed bushes, lawn, even the wide stone pathway that led up to a side entrance.

As I followed my mother through the wrought-iron gate at the side of the house, space seemed to expand, stretching first into stone arbors and bushes, a concrete drive, and then metamorphosing into an elaborate maze of rooms as we finally entered the main house. It seemed bigger than our whole apartment complex in Florida. Each time I turned a corner, I was afraid I would get lost. I felt disconnected, like the house itself. I imagined I knew how the house must feel. I thought it must be homesick too. Perhaps when we got to know each other, we could play together, this house and I. The yard seemed perfect for playing soldier—there was a pile of dirt and grass that was just right for hiding in ambush and a stack of prop rifles and army helmets was piled in a downstairs closet. A huge ornamental rug that decorated the living room floor was an ideal setting to build castles and forests of chessmen and dominos. Whole villages and towns could fit easily into its intricately woven patterns. Perhaps this house wouldn't be such a sad place after all.

Those were the days when tradesmen came to your door. I looked forward to the vegetable wagon that would come once a week with its bright array of oranges, bananas, apples— whatever fruit happened to be in season. And the Helms Bakery Man with his crisp uniform and tilted cap. And then there was the mysterious milkman who came too early in the morning to be seen, but transformed the empty bottles with their scribbled notes into shiny glass bottles of milk and cartons of cottage cheese and fresh sweet cream. My favorite playmate was a little Catholic friend who lived down the block. I don't remember her name, but her face is still quite clear in my mind, particularly the two long golden braids that hung from an always neatly groomed head. Our favorite outing was to go a small park about two blocks from my house. It had a large pond where we would catch tadpoles, fully intending to nurture them into adulthood. I don't remember what happened to them once I got them home, although I have no memory of ever seeing any frogs.

I went to public school until the fourth grade when, on top of the asthma that was always plaguing me, I acquired an unexplained fever that went on for weeks. My stepfather's first wife had been a Christian Scientist and my parents decided to send me to a Christian Science grammar school to see if that would help. I was never particularly religious, I don't think I ever really believed in God—which fit in quite well with the transcendentalism of Christian Science and its God who is never personified. I liked the new Sunday School with its snow-white walls that always looked freshly painted and its thick blue plush seats, and Berkeley Hall, my new school, with its large oval green lawn with resident ducks. And it worked. My asthma lessened to a faint occasional cough and the fever disappeared.

Berkeley Hall turned out to be the best thing about my childhood. I don't know if it was belief that healed me. It was just as likely the warmth and caring of the teachers and the freedom they allowed me to explore my creativity, encouraging me to write and play music and paint. During those years I published my first little magazine and wrote my first poem and one day when I was playing on the lawn was astonished by what I and my classmates and even the teacher on yard duty were sure was a phalanx of flying saucers. She rushed to call the newspaper, and on the evening news sightings were reported across Southern California.

To this day, even after belatedly reading reports published in the 1980s that those sightings were just military experimental planes, I'm still not sure what it was we actually saw. It wasn't those cylinder shaped objects flying noiselessly in formation across the sky, with no trail of fuel or any other visible means of propulsion, so much as a feeling that something was strange, alien, that prompted us to look up together, in wonder, at the sky.

I formally dissolved my membership in the Church at sixteen when I started smoking. (Christian Scientists are not supposed to smoke or drink.) Whoever received my heartfelt adolescent letter, realizing my age, wrote me back a very kind note asking me to reconsider, but I felt it would be hypocritical to continue. Also, at the same time I was attending Christian Science services, I was going to High Holiday services with my family. They knew what I had done—not why—and fully supported me since I was now attending public high school and had reached the dating age. There was no question in their mind that it was now time for me to be preparing for my eventual marriage to "a nice Jewish boy."

Children don't move; adults move them. Where my mother was, for me, was home. If I had been older, I might have been more impressed with our newfound fortune, but I was only four when we arrived in Los Angeles. I didn't really understand what a movie star was or what Hollywood and glamour meant. I only knew that every time it seemed like my world was settling in, becoming a comforting, a familiar place, everything would change.

To her credit, my mother did not walk into a household wanting in problems. My stepfather's first wife had, for reasons unspoken, wound up in a mental institution. My mother did try to take charge and treat my stepbrother and sister, for better or worse, as her own children. At least to my knowledge they never suffered physical abuse at her hands. I never remember her striking or even yelling at anyone, though in language and gesture she could be coldly cruel.

How to understand my mother now, so many years later, to have empathy—as the *I Ching* so aptly puts it—without losing dignity. How to picture what my mother must have looked like, felt like when young. As if somehow I could reach into my own bloodstream for an answer, knowing full well how extreme a fabrication I might be concocting, fashioned as it is from bits of photographs, rumors, innuendoes and outright lies.

My mother hated poverty. I think there was a grayness attached to her own childhood memories, to being poor, that became a metaphor for her. It wasn't until I got older that I realized how many of her choices were conditioned by that hatred.

Born Lillyn Butler in 1907 in Philadelphia, Pennsylvania, she was the only child in her family born in the U.S. The youngest of four sisters and a brother, she was short, little more than five feet tall, with blue eyes and blonde hair—a photo when she was a teenager shows her with hair so light it was almost white. Consequently, she "passed" in the days when dark Semitic looks meant danger, and "passing" she carried with her the weight of all the slurs and threats people made against Jewish people in the '20s and '30s.

She hardly ever spoke about her childhood except to say her father in "the old country" had been a renowned teacher and intellectual who, for love, had married beneath him— my grandmother was a seamstress. A lucky break since, my mother added bitterly, when the family emigrated to this country, her mother could teach him to sew, enabling him to make a living, meager as it was, for the family. Ironically, her father sewed better "than mother, made the tiniest stitches possible to imagine, and wound up finally being the one who made all the clothes for the children." Later he worked up to clerking in a drugstore, renting the top floor for his family.

I knew almost nothing about her family. She never even mentioned my grandparents' names. Only once she spoke of a missing brother who had run off at the age of fifteen because their father beat him brutally every day—not because he had caused any trouble, to make sure he didn't. She and her sisters looked for their brother for years and finally gave up, deciding he had probably lied about his age, joined the army and been killed during the First World War.

The day the telegram came announcing my grandmother's death, my mother stormed into her room. Even downstairs I could hear her opening and then slamming her desk drawer. She said only one word when she emerged from her bedroom.

"Good."

It was rumored that when she was seventeen, she had run away to be a showgirl in Florida and had married some young man who worked in a nightclub, and my grandparents had tracked her down, brought her forcibly back home, and had the marriage annulled. She never forgave them.

When my mother met my father, he was a furniture salesman at *Sterns*, a large department store in Philadelphia. He fit in

Mother: 1944/1917

well with her family, all of whom by then had comfortably entered the Jewish working class. David Luber was a handsome man in the much less muscular days of the 1920s, looked a little like Robert Taylor, and was renowned for the width and grace of his smile, and the sweetness of his disposition.

I think at the beginning they must have had fun. There are photographs of them bicycling on the boardwalk in Atlantic City, walking hand-in-hand on the beach, laughing. But people who knew her suspected she was cheating on him even then. In my mother's eyes my father had two unforgivable faults: people paid more attention to him than to her, and he had absolutely no ambition.

When they got divorced, her family never forgave her leaving a man they liked and approved of to move more than 3000 miles away to an alien world that intimidated them. His family, on the other hand, always spoke well of her. "Lillyn just had too much spirit for this place," they told me, years later, when I met what was left of them, at my father's funeral. Lillyn had spirit, but everyone loved Dave. His biggest problem was he would tell you anything to make you like him, to make things all right. It was probably why he was such a successful salesman.

In 1942, when I was three, my parents separated and my mother and I moved from my birthplace, Philadelphia, to Miami. I believed for years that we moved because I suffered from asthma, but after my mother died, I came across an album that contained a series of photos of her with a soldier with his face cut out, and I realized that she had left my father and moved south—using my illness as an excuse—to follow a man she loved. I still remember waking to the songs of troops marching to the army base close by, their voices thick in the early morning sun. During the year we lived in Miami, I often fell asleep cloaked in the artificial darkness of a "blackout," curtains drawn tight against possible harm.

It was there my mother renewed her acquaintance with Edward Sherman, my soon-to-be-stepfather. The son of a kosher butcher, he had emigrated with his family from Russia at the beginning of the twentieth century and had left home at the age of fifteen to work as a struggling actor and writer in the Jewish theater. It was on the vaudeville stage on the Atlantic City boardwalk, he discovered both his true talent as an actor's agent and Abbott and Costello, and through wit and will and a pathological ambition had brought them to Hollywood to the fame and fortune of the movie screen.

To earn money, my mother clerked in a liquor store while I was looked after by the nurse who had taken care of me as a baby and, forgoing salary, worked for room and board since she had lost her own child and in her mind and heart had adopted me—and perhaps she too had fallen under my mother's spell. She kept house while my mother played the breadwinner until my future stepfather came along and rescued my mother from her soldier and my father and the liquor store to carry her off to Hollywood and the glamour she had always dreamed of.

Where do I fit into all this? Born ten years after my parents married, I wasn't supposed to be born at all. The doctors had told my mother she had a tipped uterus and could never bear children. My first glimpse of the world came, not from the small opening between my mother's legs, but through a large gash in her belly. According to her, she hovered between life and death for four days and, thanks to me, never recovered her comely ninety-nine pound frame.

Perhaps I was that last present my mother wanted from my father before she finally left him. Or, maybe, more realistically, I reminded her time was passing, and if she wanted something different she'd better get on with it. If my stepfather was not exactly Prince Charming, at least, in her mind, he was headed in the right direction.

GLAMOUR

In 1939, six weeks after I was born, Germany attacked Poland. September 3rd, Britain and France declared war. I don't remember much of what happened those first years, I was too young. The real effects would come later for me—circled in warnings, cloaked in advice.

Rebels in their own way, my parents rejected their parents' values for the temptations of the new world. My mother and father were the only children in their respective families born in the United States. My stepfather emigrated to this country at the age of eleven. Jews were fleeing from Russia, Poland, the *pogroms*, conscription into the army, with only what they could carry on their bodies and their backs. One uncle was buried for three days under a pile of corpses, crazed with pain and fear, afraid to breathe, to show life. Stories I would hear repeatedly, sternly, as if to warn me, whenever as a child my obedience to family dogma seemed to waver. We *had* to stick together. We could depend on no one but each other.

Watch your accent, how you speak. Watch your inflection, the emotion in your words, your hands. Watch the way you walk. At their center, they will always hate you. In moments of intimacy, it will always be there. You are Jewish, a woman. What you do can turn back on your family, a whole people. Don't draw attention to yourself. Hide.

It was a lesson I learned all too well. Hiding my stepfather's mania from my mother, hiding my sexuality from almost everyone until the women's movement and gay liberation. Hiding my political activities in the left. Being afraid to voice my most intimate feelings of love—except in poems.

It is 1945. My new family is gathered around a large console radio. There is tremendous excitement. We hear a minute-by-minute report of the dropping of the first atomic bomb. Afterward I am sent to describe the event to my stepsister who has the measles, with the dual-purpose of exposing me to the disease. That was the way of it then—"getting rid of it while young."

Both events take on equal importance. They are treated the same.

Some months later, a child is ushered by her stepfather into a small room in the corner of their house, a room filled with overstuffed leather furniture, a room with no appreciable purpose carelessly tacked onto the rest of the house. The child is small and impressionable and that particular room, which always seems bathed in twilight, makes her feel suffocated. The huge (to her child's eyes) chairs are the color of quicksand, and sometimes she has dreams in which she imagines herself sinking into their murky depths, disappearing without a trace. The six-year-old is gestured into a seated position by the stranger who now calls himself her father as he draws up a chair opposite her, leans over the small coffee table that separates them, and lowering his voice to a conspiratorial whisper precedes to tell her deliberately, with hardly a trace of emotion, that she is the cause of every fight he and her mother have ever had.

What is most startling about this event is that even at six she knows it is not true. She is overwhelmed not by a sense of guilt, but with her first recognition of injustice.

That year also marked the last time I would see my biological father until my junior year in college. My stepfather legally adopted me and according to law was now my "real" father—even my birth certificate was changed.

My father faded from my life and my stepfather, "Uncle Eddie," became simply Dad.

Reading was my sanctuary, my safe haven. A private world where no one could reach me. I read everything I could get my hands on—from popular children's books of the time like *Anne of Green Gables, Daddy Longlegs, The Secret Garden, Thunderhead, My Friend Flicka* and the complete set of *Oz* books, to my mother's library of soft-core best sellers and historical novels, to the traditional classics. And comic books. I neatly sorted and catalogued each of them—Superman, Batman, Flash, Captain Marvel, the Classic Comics. But my favorites were the Oz books, even when I got older, even now.

I had a favorite fantasy based on a kingdom from *Tik-Tok of Oz* populated by the kings and queens of light and darkness who were responsible for making sure that all the lights of the universe were in good working order—daylight and candlelight, starlight, even electric light. This land which was never named was the dwelling place of the dragons who breathed firelight, including the great dragon who was the first living creature. It was a land ruled over by the Private Citizen, a great magician and the only one fit to rule because he was the only one who had no title.

I pretended I had found my way to that land on the other side of the world and made friends with the great dragons, who were sky-blue in color and set with silver scales. I became apprenticed to the Private Citizen, returning there once a year to study and work. No one at home would know anything about my secret life, would know who was responsible for the mysterious and wonderful things that would once in a while happen.

You pretended magic, I lived it. Your stepfather gave me a diamond engagement ring that glowed, yes, glowed on my finger. Sometimes I would just sit and look at it and marvel. I couldn't believe it was mine. You know we had to sell it later, when he got ill, to pay the rent and bills and buy food.

By then, I didn't care. Nobody came around anymore anyway. There was no one to see it but me.

How could you know what those early years were like? What it was to finally live in a big, open house, to have room to breathe? You grew up with everything you needed. I never had anything I needed when I was growing up. My family, all seven of us, lived in a space smaller than our living room on Bedford Drive. Even though your father and I lived in a nice apartment in Philadelphia, with him I was just like everyone else. Just getting by.

I didn't want to live the rest of my life just getting by.

How can you understand what it meant to me to be treated with deference? How could you understand what it was like to have parents who couldn't speak English, who never wanted to fit in, who never even tried? How could you understand that kind of poverty—everything dark and dull and dreary. Our clothes, our rooms, never anything bright, anything that glowed.

Hollywood was exciting. It was a brand new world.

I knew what a movie star was even if you were too young to know.

We had a party almost every week when the weather was warm. They all came to our house—Connie Haynes and Andy Russell, Lynn Bari and Peggy Ryan, William Bendix and Vaughn Monroe and Jeannie Porter. Hardly anyone remembers who they were now, but they were big stars then. Rudy Vallee and Sabu and, of course, Bud Abbott and Lou Costello. Lou dressed up like a chauffeur and drove us to the train in a limousine for our honeymoon. I have a photo of that. Can you understand that finally I was in the place I had dreamed of being all my life?

Is this her voice or mine? It is so hard to know what her voice was. We so rarely spoke.

Glamour: In myths and children's stories, a spell that wraps the worn and decayed, the ugly and evil in a mist that glitters and seduces. An illusion that sucks you into it like an incubus, draining your soul. What I do remember, Mother, is dinner table conversation about how actors' lives were constructed for them by the studios, how their lives were written into being by press agents, how almost none of it was real. How it was hidden that Lauren Bacall and Leslie Howard were Jewish. Even though many of the studio heads were Jewish, in the forties movie stars had to be Christian and white. I heard early on the "dirty secrets" everyone knows now. I knew as a teenager in the fifties that Rock Hudson was gay. My father joked about how hard it had been to train him to "speak like a man." I listened while they discussed what a crime it was that Lena Horne had to live in a trailer outside the hotel in New York she was performing at because she was black, even though it was the North and she was a big star then. How scenes with black people in them were always shot so they could be cut when the films were distributed in the South. All this from the Hollywood everyone idolized. How it was finally all as fake as the false facades on movie sets. Towns built with phony fronts with nothing inside but the wooden beams that propped them up.

What you never understood was how hard it was to eat at night listening to the way you and my stepfather spoke to each other, how your voices would become suddenly low, the way animals growl, the way animals pace, circling each other, ominous and angry. The night I heard you scream and the door slam and I found you crying on the floor of your dressing room, a room that had always scared me, lined as it was from floor to ceiling with mirrors. It seemed like there were hundreds of you lying on the floor, pounding the floor— he had left with a gun, he had threatened to kill you, to kill himself. I held you and tried to comfort you.

I was five years old.

June, 1961, three weeks after I finished school, I came home to be greeted by a psychopath who was convinced I was leaving him to run away with a secret lover. My stepfather refused to speak to me, watched me in a jealous rage whenever I left the house, peering through the green Venetian blinds, binoculars in hand.

I came home to be greeted by a mother who tersely gave me fifty dollars carefully counted out in ten dollar bills and ordered me to leave the house as soon as possible. He was her husband; she had to live with him. I was expendable. He was not.

With fifty dollars you sent me away, not asking where I was going, how I was going to get there. What was surprising is perhaps not what you did, given your history, but how little I reacted at the time. Maybe it was all I unconsciously expected from you, more likely it was because I was twenty-one years old and in my mind was already far away from home, looking eastward with no intention of looking back.

Please, try to understand. You were no longer that little baby who was a part of me. You were growing up, and I was growing old. Do you think I didn't notice how your stepfather looked at you? I didn't want him to pay attention to you, to buy you things. I wanted everything to come from me. When that failed, do you blame me for not wanting you around? You were leaving anyway. I knew that nothing could stop you. Do you think you are so different from me? I knew you would never come back. I needed you to love me. Only me. Can you understand now? I didn't need them *to love* you, *I needed* you *to love* me.

And I did, mother, I did.

A HISTORY LESSON

In 1963, my mother came East to visit her sister in Philadelphia. I had barely spoken to her since my abrupt departure from Los Angeles two years before and was dreading seeing her again.

It was a cold November morning when I met her. The air had a chill matched only by my nervousness. I couldn't tell what was causing the slight tremor in my hands, the icy wind or my apprehension. My clothes felt stiff, uncomfortable— nothing seemed to want to bend. My shoes, arms, the scarf stuffed firmly into the collar of my coat were rigid and unyielding.

My mother had taken a cab directly to Penn Station from the airport—we would take the train together to Philadelphia. I searched the crowd gathered around the Information Booth where we had agreed to meet until I spotted her. Seeing me, she waved and smiled as if our last unfortunate parting had never taken place. As much as I tried , I could not sustain my anger. Seeing her looking so small, almost frail, I felt once again that undeniable link that makes you yearn to put your arms around someone and hold them, a familiarity that cannot be denied.

In 1987, my stepbrother called me to tell me my mother had had a stroke. He said the doctors didn't expect her to survive the night. Two days later he called to tell me it seemed that she would live after all and eventually be able to regain her speech, although she would be paralyzed on her left side and, given the fact she was eighty-years-old, there was little hope for a full recovery. He wired me a ticket and I got on the next plane for California.

It was early afternoon when I arrived. It was February and unusually hot even for Los Angeles. The quick transition from a bitterly cold day in New York was difficult enough, but to make matters worse, the hospital was stifling. A nurse, short, stocky, and out-of-sorts, in answer to my inquiries told me to wait and they would wheel my mother out to me.

"It's good for the patients' morale to get them up. We try to keep them out of their rooms as much as possible."

The plural form—an institutional cliché.

After what seemed like an interminable length of time, the nurse wheeled an old woman into the waiting area. For one dreadful moment, I wasn't sure what to do. I couldn't tell if the woman sitting slumped in the wheelchair was my mother. This woman looked more like she could be my mother's mother—even then the resemblance was slight. My mother's hair was always carefully groomed and had been kept blond long after it had turned gray. This woman's hair was white, the yellowish color that white hair can turn when it isn't cared for. Her face was wrinkled and gaunt, expressionless, lacking makeup or contour. My mother was always properly "made up," even in the confines of her own home. If this *was* my mother, it would be horrible if she realized I didn't recognize her. If it wasn't my mother, it would be both embarrassing and puzzling to be embraced by a total stranger. I finally decided I would have to risk it, just in case she did belong to me, so kneeling down I took her in my arms and gently hugged the old woman who sat shriveled in a hospital wheelchair.

The next time I saw her, at my stepfather's funeral, was the last. A year later, she died from a heart attack. It was New Year's Eve. I had no money, and my stepbrother considered it a waste of his to buy me another ticket— according to Jewish custom she had to be buried almost immediately, and since she certainly wouldn't know the difference, he couldn't see the point in my making the long trip home.

So the woman who had given me life passed out of it, as ghostly a presence in death as she had been for me alive.

Two years after my mother died, my biological father died. At his funeral I stood once again a stranger. His wife told me he was buried with the photos of his two children—a half-brother I had only seen twice before and me. If true, it was the closest to him I ever got.

I grew up in a home that tried to emulate an America that was alien to them. My parents weren't rich, they were poor people with money. As their fortunes diminished over the years, the years themselves changed. From the glamour of the forties to the repressive conservatism of the fifties into the corporate sixties, their homes got smaller and more modest. As each rise in fortune had been accompanied by a newer and bigger house, so each fall was signaled by selling one house for money and buying another cheaper one, each one in a less prestigious neighborhood, until finally, instead of buying, they were renting. Gone by 1950 were the limousine and chauffeur, the swimming pool and the big parties that had first enticed my mother to California until finally, when I visited my parents in 1975, they were living in a small apartment—not much different from my biological father's in Camden, New Jersey that my mother had so disdained—wearing polyester clothes and looking very much like the photos of my mother's working-class brothers and sisters. A box of cigars and a few pieces of silver were the only remnants of a more affluent age.

Mine was a family that made a virtue of forgetfulness, that hungered to erase any semblance of their past, anything that would remind them of what they had left. I only know the names of two of my mother's four sisters. Where they were born, when they died, I don't know. I don't know the names of my father's brothers or where they were born, or when and how they died. I don't know my grandparents' names. I remember meeting my mother's parents once when I was four. They didn't speak English. They were very old, and their house smelled like crackers and warm milk. I remember meeting my father's father in Atlantic City. He was eighty or eighty-five and lived in a single-room-occupancy in a small hotel a block from the beach. If I ever knew his name, I have forgotten.

Diaspora means being uprooted, torn up by the roots. Mine was a personal *Diaspora* which left me in search of origins, a family, because a home, a history, is not found in places alone, it is found with people. And so I began my search to find and refind those people I could call "home." A search that obsesses me to this day.

NEW YORK 1961 – 1967:
The Early Years

Years before, the pain. And now, a line, circling into a hand, pointing into space...

"ON THE ROAD"

The highway was taut, thick, cramped, like an abused muscle, hot and volatile. I had always thought of heat as static, but this heat was mobile, pushing me relentlessly forward while simultaneously forming an almost impenetrable barrier—squeezing me mercilessly between the future and the past. All the while, an endless collage of used-car lots, drive-in theaters, low one-story office buildings, sped past our open car windows, the noise of the road drowning any attempt at conversation, the sky yellow with dust and exhaust fumes, typical of the borders of western cities, California, Nevada, Utah, the first stage of our journey east.

I had set out from Berkeley with Sylvia, another friend, Carol, and Carol's dog Siegfried barely one week after my forced exit from Los Angeles to embark on a three-week exodus across the United States, northern route, which was to end for me at least the 1950s mythic glamour of being "on the road."

We had gotten our car through an announcement in a San Francisco newspaper advertising free rental and an allowance for gas if we drove it east to its owner. It was a '56 Ford two-door painted a dusty brownish yellow with black plastic seat covers which fit perfectly both the landscape and our mood. Besides two or three dents in the hood and a back bumper that tilted slightly to the left, it seemed fit enough to get us where we wanted to go.

In the middle of downtown Sacramento, less than three hours from our starting point, the car broke down for the first time. The gas station mechanic said it was a minor repair and one hour and twenty-five dollars later we were finally on our way. To avoid the heat and save money—we had no more than a couple hundred dollars between us—we planned to sleep by the side of the road during the day and travel by night. The second day out we discovered it was too hot to

67

sleep during the day, so after almost forty-eight hours taking turns driving and sleeping in a moving car, we decided to rent a room for eighteen-fifty for the afternoon at a rundown motel which advertised itself as *AIR CONDITIONED* in huge letters in green neon framed in a garish orange and rose.

A women who looked as old as the faded blue-striped house dress she was wearing barely looked at us as we registered and paid for our room. She informed us obliquely as soon as she had collected our money and locked it in a large steel box that the "A/C is temporarily out of order. We're waiting for a repair man. It should be fixed in an hour or so."

We were too exhausted to protest, or move on, so the three of us and Siegfried, who was suffering as much as we were, spread ourselves out on a lumpy double bed that filled up almost the entire room—the bed wasn't large, the room was small. We assumed every conceivable combination of positions, trying not to touch each other, or to let any part of our body touch another part. Not because we were inhibited, because we were hot.

Carol finally spread herself out parallel to the bottom edge of the bed with her dog, and I fell into a fitful sleep, only to wake up less than an hour later, dizzy and nauseous. I spent the better part of the rest of the afternoon throwing up from the heat in a bathroom hardly big enough to contain both me and the toilet.

We left in early evening, just as the sun was exuding a color that made the sky look morbidly like the color of our vehicle. In the middle of the night, in the middle of a two-block town, in the middle of nowhere, our car, which had begun sputtering and smoking again, finally stopped dead just as we made it to the parking area of a deserted gas station. We couldn't believe our luck and were about to get out and try to find help when our stalled vehicle was surrounded by a gang of six or seven teenagers with drawn knives who looked deceptively like stereotypical suburban teens. They began shouting insults and banging on the car windows, which were now tightly locked, with their fists and beer cans.

Carol kept trying to push her frantically barking dog at the window to scare them away. But the dog was obviously as frightened as we were and hardly a convincing deterrent.

Just when it seemed the gang might succeed in breaking in, we were saved by the local sheriff who drove up wearing a tin six-pointed-star badge and, bantering with "the guys" like it was one big joke, suggested they let "them girls" alone. He waited for a few minutes until they vanished as suddenly as they had appeared and assured us with a huge grin that they were really harmless and we would have no more trouble and anyway what were nice girls like us doing in the middle of nowhere, in the middle of the night. The whole scenario resembled a Grade B movie, but it wasn't funny and it wasn't fiction. The sheriff suggested we stay put, since there was no where else to go, and wait until the station opened in the morning.

Almost delirious at this point with panic and fatigue, I felt as if my body and the body of the car had somehow changed places, that I was a great yellow mass squatting immobile in the center of the now-deserted gas station. Everything around me seemed lifeless, inert, even the bodies of my sleeping companions. I had no idea where I was headed, intellectually, emotionally, or geographically. I had the horrible feeling that we had become absorbed by the steel that enclosed us like a distorted 50s beat version of Sleeping Beauty, doomed to lie forever in a castaway automotive coffin. But this tale had no Prince Charming to break the spell, just a gang of bloodthirsty teenagers, like the white power gang that had confronted me and my friends in Berkeley, ready to commit violence at a moment's notice.

The next morning, as soon as our car was fixed, we drove north until we arrived at Glacier National Park. Reveling in the blasts of fresh Canadian air, we spread our sleeping bags on the hard ground next to the car—we had no camping equipment—feeling safe for the first time since we left Berkeley. We swam the week away in the icy lake waters formed by the runoff of a great Canadian glacier until we felt we had finally washed off the days of heat and fear that had thus far accompanied us, welcoming the huge green canopy of mountain branches that sheltered us from intermittent rain, relishing the easy camaraderie of the communal cooking and toilet facilities that serviced the park.

It was the first time in what seemed like an interminable trip that I began to believe I might actually reach New York. I had no idea what to expect even though Diane's letters had been long and rich in description. I felt I was caught up in a rite of passage, a purification, bathing myself every afternoon in the frigid waters that flowed south into the park, washing off the remnants of my trip home, my mother's rejection, my stepfather's insanity.

I celebrated my twenty-second birthday with Sylvia and Carol, sitting in a small restaurant on the Canadian side of the park, drinking wine and watching the stillness of the waters, the air so clear and chill it acted as a magnifying lens, making everything sharp and close, time momentarily on hold.

Finally we could delay no longer. Driving south back into the United States, we now found ourselves surrounded by the level terrain of the great plains stretching around us for more than a thousand miles, a huge flat circle, rimmed by thin stripes of alternating lightning, sun, clouds, and long thin shadows falling from sky to ground that Sylvia explained to me was rain. It felt like we were moving forward through the emptiness toward an inexplicable horizon that seemed to recede from us as fast as we moved toward it, the only possible alternative being to eventually drive over the edge of the world.

It was easy to believe in that place that the world *was* flat, that the ancients had been right all along.

At five o'clock in the morning, we finally left the plains.

Halfway down one nondescript mountain road our headlights blew out, leaving us in almost total darkness. The stars had dimmed; the sun had not yet begun to rise. We were afraid to stop for fear a car speeding along in the dark would back-end us and throw us over the mountain ledge. We were equally afraid to go on for fear we'd drive ourselves over the ledge.

Carol got out of the car and holding on to the hood of the car with one hand and a flashlight with the other guided us slowly along the narrow path until an hour later the sun finally rose enough for us to see where we were going.

Exhausted, we gave up "doing it on our own" and picked up two young sailors somewhere in the vicinity of Chicago to help us drive—only to be stopped by the highway patrol for speeding. Checking their IDs, the cops discovered they were AWOL. It took us two solid hours and a lot of ingenuity to convince the police we didn't know them, had no idea they were AWOL and continue on our way.

When we landed finally, drained and filthy, at Sylvia's house in Brooklyn, I called Diane and made arrangements to meet her at her apartment on Bank Street the next evening and go with her to meet the poets at a coffee shop restaurant named after the famous cafe in Paris—*Les Deux Megots*.

THE DEUX MEGOTS

On hot July mornings, Seventh Street between First and Second Avenue is still punctuated with beer cans, newspapers, and bright bits of garbage festering in the summer heat—a city feast for pigeons, sparrows, and rodents—both squirrels and rats. On Sunday, the morning stillness is broken precisely at 10:45 by the sound of a single church bell summoning parishioners to morning prayer. Its mellow solitary tones are tedious, but strangely comforting, in stark contrast to the sharp quick echoes of crowd-filled Saturday nights. It is amazing how little Seventh Street has changed in the last forty years. But maybe that is because I live here, and like with a person you see every day, the changes over time are slight and therefore barely noticeable.

In the early Sixties, when I first came to inhabit what was then known as the Lower East Side, I was unaware consciously of the forces that drove me and the world around me. It was a period empty of notions and labels. I had neither the time nor inclination to analyze and plan. I moved almost in a state of grace.

Most experiences as they are lived claim an importance beyond their real significance. Each new friend, new place, new love seems spectacular at the moment of inception. In retrospect, few stand the test of time. Among those I can count without equivocation: the night I first entered the Deux Megots. The Deux Megots was a coffee house run by Mickey Ruskin, who would later own The Ninth Circle and then Max's Kansas City, famous as a hangout for Andy Warhol and a center for punk rock—its music space inaugurated in 1970 by The Velvet Underground. Ruskin had bought the Deux Megots with his partner Bill Makey only two months before I arrived—most of the poets who gathered there to read had first found each other at The Tenth Street Coffee House, the space he had owned previously.

I don't remember in detail the first evening I went to the Deux Megots. Memory is not consistent, is not based on a compilation of facts, but on closeness and caring, frustration and desire. The Deux Megots was more than a place to me, it was an event, and as such a description of it in physical terms has to be liberally accented by an emotion and expectation that have not left me to this day.

Now a second-hand clothing store, the building on Seventh Street which housed the Deux Megots is still fronted by double windows, a large tree hiding the entrance. A small single door opens onto a medium-sized room. In its coffee house days, the room was partitioned by wooden banisters separating some rectangular and a few large round wooden tables, maybe a dozen in all. The wall to the left as you entered, where the poets read, was stripped to its original brick. The food was good, the special a decent rib steak, bone in, for about $1.75. It must have been fairly smoky since, in those days, most of us smoked. The lighting was soft, comfortable, soothing. Even with the many incarnations the space has gone through—from coffee house, to macrobiotic restaurant, to used bookstore, to a place of last resort for second-hand clothes—the shape of the room is unchanged, the original brick wall is still there. And if I look hard enough, closely enough, I can even now see the flickering shapes of the poets, projected by loving memory, moving behind the windows.

Over there, on the left, by the window, is Allen Katzman. Allen, with his twin brother Don, edits Hespiridian Press. He will later go on to be one of the founders and editors of *The East Village Other*, a counter-culture newspaper of the Sixties. He is pacing the floor with that odd bent walk of his, toes pointed inward, intently smoking a cigarette, and thinking about—who knows what? And there, beside him, trying to get his attention is Robert Nichols, straight and tall, with a head of hair that always looks like he has just come in from outdoors, the wind permanently blowing through it. Carol Bergé, unusually quiet, sits at the table closest to the readers. She is small and intense, with an infectious laugh and volatile energy and a sure staccato in her voice that carries into her poems, spilling over into a low vocalized choral accompaniment underscoring work she likes. Carol will be responsible for introducing me to Margaret Randall, the editor—with her husband Sergio Mondragon—of the bilingual literary journal *El Corno Emplumado* published in Mexico City. An introduction which will result in trips to Cuba and Nicaragua and a whole new direction and commitment in my life.

Hidden behind the stacks of paper he is shuffling on one of the wooden banisters that breaks the room into discrete sections, Howard Ant, who runs the Monday night open reading, is going over the list of poets who have signed up to read. Along with Ree Dragonette, Howard was one of the original founders of the poetry readings at the Tenth Street Coffeehouse. Ed Sanders, the poet/activist who will become widely known in the early Seventies with the publication of his book on Charles Manson, *The Family*, is holding the latest edition of his journal *Fuck You/A Magazine of the Arts* and conferring with Jackson Mac Low and John Harriman, fellow activists, while Barbara Holland, preparing to read, poses stiffly in an ankle-length cloth coat. From the neck down she looks like she could have walked out of an early 1950s magazine advertisement—until you pan up to her stricken face, an appropriate accompaniment to her raspy voice and poems of terror and gore.

I see myself now, twenty-two and not a little frightened. I have a batch of new poems under my arm and tonight will be the first time I will read them. Each poet is allotted three poems or five minutes after which audience comments are invited—enough to make anyone nervous—and I am young, both in years and experience. Allen waves me over to his table. He is now seated with Carol and his brother Don. I look around for Diane, but she hasn't arrived yet.

Jerry Rothenberg, Robert and Jobie Kelly, Dave Antin and Armand Schwerner, editors of Hawk's Well and Trobar Press, sit around one of the large round tables engaged in a heated discussion with Paul Blackburn about the Deep Image and their bookstore, The Blue Yak. Marguerite Harris, gesturing adamantly, is pontificating about some minor poetic conundrum. Maggie, as everyone calls her, delights in reminding us at every possible opportunity that she makes her living playing benevolent grandmothers on TV commercials—in direct contrast to her real personality, always acting, as she does, as if the poetry world were her own private preserve.

At the back of the cafe, slouching against the kitchen counter, Taylor Mead, long before Andy Warhol fame, waits nonchalantly for his turn to read. Taylor is the most openly homosexual poet in the group and manages with his wry sense of humor to be funny and serious in a minimum of words, poking fun indiscriminately at everything and everyone including himself.

"Darling," he drawls, when it is finally his time to read, "If you don't dig it, lay down your shovel." "I'm bisexual," he continues. "I like tall men and short men." He finishes with a flourish, flashing the half smile that for him replaces a grin. I join the general applause, amused, but also vaguely uneasy, confused as I am about my own sexuality.

Finally Diane arrives with Ted Enslin, who is just back from a visit to Maine, and greeting us, sits down between Jerry Rothenberg and Robert Kelly. They are joined by Jerry and Elaine Bloedow who enter close behind her—Jerry striding handsome into the Deux Megots in a leather motorcycle jacket, Elaine by his side with short curly blonde hair cut almost to her scalp, and tiger eyes.

Completing the assembly, scattered around the remainder of the room in various positions of reading, meditating,

Bridge Theater Reading: Robert Nichols, Susan Sherman, Allen Katzman.
Photo: Karl Bissinger

editing, and/or gesturing in animated conversation are two dozen or more poets and writers and artists.

One of the poems I have clutched so tightly against me is a prose poem. I had been used to writing a kind of tight skeletal imagist poem, left over from workshops in San Francisco and Berkeley. The images sometimes worked and my work was becoming more finely crafted, but much too abstract. Since the long line used by Allen Ginsberg didn't appeal to me either, Ted encouraged me to experiment with a prose line using my own voice. The result was a prose poem called, aptly enough, "Genesis," inspired by an early memory of my father coming to visit me in the hospital after I had my tonsils out. I was barely three. They used ether in those days for anesthesia and I remember crying, and then something put over my face, and wave after wave of color, and I woke up and my father was standing there with a toy he had brought me, a tin solder that played a small tin drum.

Howard Ant finally calls my name and I get up and with that memory of color and darkness, I begin:

Night—an interim, a point in time. Along this line, straight, geometrical, existing only in length, in one dimension, my memories exist.

All nights placed together. A wall—long, high, without depth. A slide, curved in space. A steel soldier jerking its arms mechanically against a small steel drum.

Never remembering after that one day. Red. Blue. And the sound of the drum, over and over...

Genesis. A beginning. *To know. The beginning always continues.* A new form, and finally words come.

*Lost in images, I walk the borders of days. Words weld
together, indistinguishable from the sound of my mind
weaving pictures, ideas, memories.*

*Everything—just to keep order. Just to preserve
stability among the flashes, the arrows of stimuli, that vibrate
through my spine. How the baby cries, unable
to find an outline among the shapes that threaten it.
How the consciousness groans, forced to define paths,
force directions, dictate systems.*

*And for one instant, when the process stops. Lost in a blur
of color, sound, echoes, words, voices, motion.*

That long night in Berkeley on psilocybin. The room
reduced to lines and color. I had survived that night and now,
using the images of night, I would break through again.

Ted nods his approval when I return to the table. He
encourages me to send "Genesis" to his friend Cid Corman
who is publishing a new series of his magazine, *Origin*.
Corman responds with a long, detailed letter accusing me of
being callous and misguided because of the lines: *It is evil
that brings us into contact with the world. Violence and
conflict. The rest is solitude and the distance sensed in a
dream.*

Upset, angry, and intimidated by Corman's comments, I
put his letter in a drawer. Ted thinks his letter encouraging,
an open invitation to correspond, but I don't have the heart
for it. "Genesis" was the first writing I had done which was
so intensely personal. I just couldn't retreat into intellectually
analyzing or debating material I was just beginning to grapple
with emotionally.

It was a time when I believed. Not only in the power and
sanctity of the poem, but in all things mysterious and
mystical—particularly in the Tarot and the Chinese Book of

Changes, the *I Ching*. One night Robert Kelly introduced me
to a new oracle—*Kenkyusha*. A Japanese-English Dictionary.
Kenkyusha's many definitions reading like short poems, the
trick was to ask a question and open it at random. I still have
Kenkyusha. It is weather-beaten and dog-chewed, lacking part
of its spine, but the inside is intact, having successfully
survived a week in the freezer where I put it for punishment
when I was angered by one of its observations and couldn't
figure out any other way to torture an oracle-book.

I pull it out now for the first time in years, to see what it
has to say.

Susan (me): a extradition treaty; delivered, transferred...
Sense, [=wisdom] comes with age. We must modulate our voice
according to the size of the room.

How like *Kenkyusha* to still be lecturing me.

Carol Bergé: cold water ablutions... a small dwelling with land
attached.
Diane Wakoski: ...a steel helmet, a trench helmet. a shrapnel
helmet, a battle bowler, a tin hat.
Theodore Enslin: ...taking a leaf out of a wise man's book.
carrying knowledge into new fields.
Allen Katzman: He disclaims his own merit in favor of others.
Jerry Bloedow: ...loosened hair.
Robert Kelly: ...arrowroot-starch paste.
Robert Nichols: ...a tremendous clash like a hundred claps of
thunder.
Marguerite Harris: ...world conquest.

I don't know whether pure chance (if you believe in such
a thing) has pictured my friends then or now, who these poets
actually were or how I saw them.

Poets on the Beach/Early 1960s. Clockwise from top: Jerry and
Elaine Bloedow, Diane Wakoski, Ted Enslin, Jerry Bloedow.
Photo: Susan Sherman

It was at the Deux Megots I began to learn to write, to translate my passion into words, to translate my world into something I could grow into and beyond. I was forced to learn fast because I was so far behind—there was so much I had to read and speak and live and understand.

In retrospect I'm not sure whether any of us really heard each other past the surface and the craft. Looking back now, I wonder how much we got past the sound of the "voice," the pattern of words, the "image" to what the individual who was speaking was trying to articulate. How much we listened to what was unspoken, past the boundaries, the cerebral fences that dictated even in that bohemian context what was expected in both our poems and our lives.

Not what we were, but what we could become.

This, of course, was compounded for me by my being gay and by the way I dealt with, or, more accurately, didn't deal with it. It was 1961, and I had no knowledge of the "queer" world beyond the male world which had nothing to do with me. I didn't understand that judgments could be made about a poem outside the poem. I didn't understand that how a young woman was supposed to think and act was as important as the words she spoke, the thoughts she articulated. Robert Kelly once gave me the dubious compliment of remarking that intellectually I thought like a man—which was fine, as long as I kept it to myself and continued sleeping with men as well as women and writing with the baroque and/or male-centered images expected of a woman poet.

I believed that poetry and poets were supposed to be beyond gender and race and background and religion, somewhere in the ethereal world of intellectual ambiguity— outside of self and time.

To put it quite simply, a lot of the time I just didn't get it.

That being said, those days were characterized by a genuine love of that special presence characterized by the spoken and written word.

From the first night I entered the Deux Megots and for

many years afterward, the poets and friends I met there would form the nexus from which my life would radiate. But there was one aspect of my life no one could fill. It was a place I had to uncover and learn to deal with alone.

"COMING OUT"

The old woman's skin was soft. Her breasts were round and inviting beneath the fragile transparency of her nightgown, as they rose and fell, swelled by sleep, promising refuge, safety, a place of solace and security against the fear that propelled the child into the night.

Now, years later, reaching out, a young woman is startled by a sudden feeling of desire and with desire, revulsion, and with that recognition the old woman's body fades from her dream, dissolves,

and in her place, a gigantic clock appears, with a second hand that hums as it moves, each moment vibrating with a distinct tone. And as the girl watches, the second hand slows and the distance between seconds widens

until it becomes large enough to contain her.

Touching Sylvia's face, her arms, tentatively, but without fear, the passion growing from within, extending out through my fingers, every pore of my body, the way she smells, smooth as the hollow between her cheek and eye, as I reach to touch it, rest my face in it, her smell warm, like our last day in Berkeley, bright, but still cool, both of us anxious to leave, to meet our future, but even so holding back, taking in the last few moments of lingering heat, the summer day slipping into night, the way her glance rests on me now, as I rest on her, the closeness of her, a respite from the heaviness of the humid New York July afternoon, from past months' longing, the touch of her breasts, her legs, reaching slowly, hesitantly, between her legs, her skin warm as the scent of her cheek, the curve behind her ear, brushing against her hand, as she reaches down, between my knees, my thighs, touching me as I touch her, our hands, our lips, in unison, moist, probing inward, searching, my hands beginning to tremble, alive with anticipation, with wonder, as I bury myself deeper and deeper into her, as she discovers me, my most hidden place.

After all these months of anxiety and waiting, unsure, afraid, how could it be so simple? This act of making love.

Even with men I knew and liked, sex had almost always made me feel as if I had lost a part of myself, the way a bar of soap is gradually worn away, the cover of a favorite book. That afternoon with Sylvia and all the afternoons and evenings with her that were to follow evoked sensations that were different, harder to pin down, define. It was like being fourteen again, sneaking off after school, riding one of those old buses to the Santa Monica Pier, basking in the glitz and noise of the bingo parlor, the mocking laughter of the grotesque purple and turquoise lady who decorated the doors of the Fun House warning away the timid, the wonder of the antigravity machine, its circle of people flattened tight against the sides of the whirling sphere, and then, every sense strained to the limit, counting out carefully stashed change to buy cotton candy, pink and sticky, and running with it through the sand, feet bare, feeling the water slide between my toes, seductive, trying to coax me in, half the fun coming from the danger, from doing something no one would ever know about, something private in a world where everything was open to prying eyes, something that was glorious and free.

Making love with Sylvia that afternoon in July in Brooklyn in her parents' apartment had been like that, like being fourteen again and free.

Perhaps it was because she was my friend and we genuinely liked each other, or perhaps it was because she was a woman, or simply because she was who she was, that what startled both of us was not difference, but familiarity. All we questioned was why we had waited so long. We weren't in love, but we were attracted to one another, and we were curious—and ready.

It was a time when I could separate sex and love, or more precisely, it was a time when the two had not yet come together for me, so I had no memories to hang on to, no wish to repeat. With Sylvia, even though the sex was intoxicating, passionate, it did not fill my imagination. It might have been because neither of us were ready yet to give ourselves so completely to another person or because we were both still seeing men and not ready to make that kind of commitment. Sylvia was planning to go back to graduate school in Berkeley and I would be moving into Manhattan.

Or perhaps the real reason was because I was deeply engrossed in my work, with a whole new life opening before me. My true love was with a future I had yet to conceive. I was twenty-two and the world was before me, open now to possibilities I could barely begin to comprehend. What I discovered that afternoon with Sylvia was intoxicating, daring, exciting, but I had no sense that it would drastically change the course of my life. It would be years before I would seriously invite my relationships with women into the rest of my world.

Sylvia and I had had one encounter before in Berkeley that had almost led to a sexual relationship. One night we had been innocently enough sitting on her bed/couch with another student Don, a friend of hers, when they started kissing and he started kissing me and then I started kissing Sylvia and pretty soon Don was getting less and less attention until it became painfully obvious that he really was only there so Sylvia and I could be together without admitting what was going on. From then on Sylvia avoided me until we found ourselves alone in her house in Brooklyn, in bed, finally talking about what had happened, laughing, wondering aloud to each other what it would be like if we finished what we had started so many months before. And then just as easily as we spoke, we slipped into each other's arms, and for the first time for either of us, made love to another woman. Over the weeks, our relationship became physically more and more intense. Something had opened in us.

Sylvia's mother liked me. I was a nice Jewish girl who appreciated her cooking. I was quiet and respectful. The first night I was there she cooked me a baked chicken dinner with a slice of icy cantaloupe for desert. I couldn't remember the last time I had eaten such a good meal or when I had felt so at home. I liked her too. I also liked her daughter. When Sylvia's parents weren't home, we smoked "grass" and made love. One night her parents came home unexpectedly when we were in Sylvia's bed together, holding each other. I was terrified, but they thought nothing of it. What was between us was so out of their range of possibility that it never occurred to them that we were more than two friends sharing the secrets of friends, as girls might do, in the night.

Finding a vacant apartment in Manhattan, even in those days, was no easy matter. Robert Nichols, hearing of my need to find a place to stay in the city while I was trying to find an apartment and a job, even though he hardly knew me, kindly offered to let me use his basement office/studio on Bank Street while he was on vacation. It was a spare but comfortable room with a box-spring in the corner and a mattress in a closet in the hall, which he was appalled to find out on returning I had never found. I had spent three weeks sleeping on the open metal springs, with only a sheet between me and their relentless coils.

By the end of August, 1961, I finally settled into an apartment on Suffolk Street about a half block from Delancy, in the heart of the Lower East Side, a subway stop from the Deux Megots. It was $40 a month, two rooms, newly painted a pale blue, a five-story walk-up in a well-tended building in a very seedy neighborhood. I inherited it from a couple who were in jail for selling large quantities of marijuana.

I found work ghostwriting for $60 a week at the Daniel Mead Literary Agency. Prospective writers would send in their manuscripts and receive a letter back saying the agency would send their material out, but it would need a little "editing" first. One week I did over $2000 of work billed to the author for my usual $60. I don't know how many of the finished manuscripts actually were sent out—Mead was investigated later by the Attorney General's office. When he wasn't around we would make sure that manuscripts from people obviously too poor to afford editing services would be "rejected." My new job and my new apartment seemed like the height of luxury after living in Bob Nichols' studio, sustaining myself basically on two eight-cent rolls and a couple of eggs a day when I couldn't get meals from generous friends.

I finally got my "two weeks' notice" a year later, one week before my vacation was due. Furious, I packed up my small box of belongings and left on the spot leaving a more furious Daniel Mead literally foaming at the mouth. He had thought I would stay until I could be replaced.

I continued seeing Sylvia, although it became much more difficult now that I was living in Manhattan. It was in October, 1962, the week of the Cuban missile crisis that I began to understand how important my relationship with her had become. The night Kennedy gave his ultimatum to Khrushchev there was a general feeling of doom. People roamed the streets. No one wanted to go home. The sidewalks were crowded. The bars. I could hardly believe that under the circumstances I was home in bed with the flu. What might be my last week on earth would be spent sneezing and taking massive doses of aspirin and boiling hot lemonade, coughing my fear into large white squares of Kleenex. Fear of the bomb in those years was so great that one night when my Japanese paper lantern fell from the light bulb overhead sending streams of bright white light into the apartment, without thinking I dove under the bed for cover.

All I could think of that night in October was Sylvia, lying in her arms, forgetting everything else around me, the way only being with her could make me forget, her body blocking out the terror of the events unfolding around us.

Shortly after that, I met a young woman named Norma. She was very attractive and high-spirited. She was in the process of breaking up with her current lover, and one night she invited me over to dinner and suggested I spend the night.

I agreed and our relationship began.

Over the space of the next few weeks I began seeing Norma more and Sylvia less. Sylvia was getting ready to return to California and, in any case, our relationship had always seemed temporary.

How did Sylvia feel about all this? At the time I took it for granted she felt the same way I did. The difference between then and now is that now I would think to ask.

THE POETS

If Allen Katzman was tall and broad-shouldered, Theodore Enslin was lean and muscular. I think of urban settings when I think of Allen, and of massive trees, wilderness and winter when I think of Ted. Although Ted's body was in Manhattan, his heart was always in his beloved Maine. He delighted in telling me tall tales of his life on the mountain—chopping his own wood, living without electricity and running water, hiking long miles for even the smallest necessity. Stories I naturally believed to the last detail, until a friend of his informed me his mountain house, although rough, was a bit more comfortable than Ted let on.

Those first months in Manhattan, I couldn't bear the hours between four and six in the afternoon when the light began to fail, or the middle of the night when it was silent and I was alone. Often I couldn't sleep until the sun came up. One week Ted met me at my job almost every day to escort me home.

Afraid of losing contact. As if gravity had begun to fail and at any moment I would shoot straight up, cut off from anything that had ever grounded me, secured me in place.

Ted got great pleasure out of teasing me as I sat in my small fifth-floor walk-up rear-of-the-building rooms, terrified by lightning and thunder, a phenomenon I had rarely experienced in California. Working by candlelight, I would sit with all the lights out, wearing a pair of rubber-soled sneakers. He always answered my panicked phone calls by rushing over to "comfort" me. He would usually wind up by telling me his favorite lightning stories. One night I listened in disbelief as he told me with great gusto about lightning he had heard of that bounced through open windows like deadly electric sagebrush. Acting out each gesture, he added gleefully he had a friend who loved to open the window in a just such a storm and yell into the sky, "Rain! Rain!" Which was all well and good, except the thought of an electric spark the size of a large football bouncing through my window wasn't exactly comforting.

Ted was thirty-five when I first met him. A musician before he started writing poetry, he had studied under Nadia Boulanger, the famous pianist and teacher. His profound connection to music carried over into his work. His poetry was permeated with a strong, complex but nonintrusive rhythm, lean and muscular and direct as he was himself. As Ted, the person, served as a supportive presence in my life, his poetry was a constant source of inspiration. He directed me away from the overly abstract language I had been using to lived detail—not dry in substance, but rich in description and metaphor.

Ted introduced me to his good friend Denise Levertov, a well known poet and one of the few women represented in the Donald Allen anthology, *The New American Poetry,* which was published in 1960 and was the *de facto* bible of the "new" poetry. Denise was poetry editor of *The Nation* and published some of my poems there and sent others to *Poetry* (Chicago)—one of the most prestigious journals in which to be published at the time. She also published one of my poems in *The Poetry Pilot,* the Academy of American Poets' newsletter.

I seemed right on track to solidifying my poetic reputation, but shortly afterwards Denise and I had a parting of the ways—quite possibly due to an incident that took place at a benefit reading for the Greenwich Village Peace Center.

My hands were perspiring so badly I could hardly hold my poems. I tried to focus on the words and not think about anything else—it wouldn't do to show I was so nervous. Here I was reading with Allen Ginsberg, and I had only been writing for a short time, and the poem I had picked to read was new, untried, and Denise Levertov was there, and reading also. Grace Paley and Bob Nichols had believed in me enough to ask me to read, and I didn't want to let them down. I was excited. I was scared. I wanted to run out of the room. I couldn't wait for my turn.

I would be reading a poem I had written for Norma— without the dedication. Exactly one week before, while we were making love, we had connected in a way that was entirely new to me. For that one moment, the undercurrent of guilt that still plagued me when I made love with a woman had disappeared. Later the same evening, as Norma slept, a poem began to take form. It was that poem, "The Meeting," I was about to read before all these friends and strangers:

> *To touch your face*
> *To touch your arms*
> *To touch your waist*
> *To touch your thighs*
>
> *To touch your sex*
>
> *To hold it soft against my cheek*
> *To breathe it slow against my lips*
> *To hold you close against my breast*
>
> *My love...*

An understanding so tenuous, fragile, a connection so easily broken.

> *I would hold you gently*
> *Throw myself against you as*
> *the rain Talk to you of*
> *small things As you would*
> *touch a child Or yourself*
> *small and vulnerable to even*
> *the slightest breath.*

To be able to reach out, to make contact, to open out, to connect.

> *No longer afraid The touch of you deeper*
> *than any fear Deeper than your naked form*
> *The single syllable of your name*
>
> *As I touch your body*
> *As I touch the earth*
> *As I touch this paper*
> *As I touch each word*
>
> *It is everywhere This night and the*
> *outline of our form As we are together*
> *Without boundary Without dimension*
>
> *As I touch the depth of you*
> *My love*

There was loud applause. I sat down relieved, happy to be able to relax and enjoy the rest of the reading, when Denise turned to me with a puzzled look and said, "What strange images for a woman to use."

To which Ginsberg commented wryly, "That's because she's gay."

I was so startled by the unexpectedness of his comment I hardly noticed Denise's reaction, except that she got very quiet. I didn't say anything, neither did she. I knew she believed, like many others, that Ted and I were a couple—a convenient idea I did nothing to dispel. I wasn't even aware that Ginsberg knew about my relationships with women. At the time I was quite friendly with Peter Orlovsky and might have mentioned something to him. Or maybe it was more common knowledge than I thought.

Nothing more was said. The evening went on as if nothing had happened.

A few weeks later when I sent Denise a new batch of poems—I hadn't heard anything from her since the benefit— I got a note back from her that she was disappointed in my work, it seemed to her I was basically always writing about the same subject. She never mentioned what that "subject" was. I didn't understand.

Or maybe I understood only too well.

That was the end of my contact with Denise until many years later. She would become one of the American poets actively involved in anti-war and political protest. In the Seventies, we read together again, different people in a different world. In 1975, she was responsible for publishing my poem, "Amerika," an extremely radical poem, in the *American Poetry Review.* But I can only guess what the loss of her patronage during those important early years had meant.

I originally met Allen Ginsberg, Peter Orlovsky, and Gregory Corso at the Metro Café where the poetry readings moved in 1963. At the end of 1962, after Mickey Ruskin, one of the two owners of the Deux Megots, left to open The Ninth Circle and then Max's Kansas City, the atmosphere of the Deux Megots cooled to poetry, and we moved from one place to another until we finally settled in at our new location—a cafe/ restaurant on Second Avenue between Ninth and Tenth Streets run by Moe and Cindy Margulies.

Moe also showed films at the Metro and sold antiques— the large side room was filled with old furniture—and a friend of his specialized in and sold old comic books. The Metro, like the Deux Megots, was a place you could go and sit and have an inexpensive meal or a cup of coffee. I spent most of my free time there, since I was living in the neighborhood, and became quite friendly with Moe and Cindy.

The Metro was a larger space than the Deux Megots—over a hundred people could be squeezed in if necessary, and it often was. Carol Bergé, Allen Katzman, and I ran the Monday night open readings and Paul Blackburn ran the Wednesday night feature. By 1963, the word was out and the readings were packed. Many visiting artists, writers, and musicians, including William Burroughs and Bob Dylan, passed through the Metro's doors.

The readings often seemed endless, lasting until one or two o'clock in the morning. Anyone who wanted to read could, and did—from the most traditional kind of rhymed poetry (which brought the biggest guffaws, particularly from Paul Blackburn) to the most avant-garde, from one-liners designed to elicit laughs to work that was completely uncharacterizable. Moe would frequently worry because the sidewalk outside the café was so crowded with people lined up, demanding to get in. It was hardly a money-maker for him, the price of admission was the price of the mandatory cup of coffee or tea—twenty-five cents.

The poetry generally followed in the tradition of male-centered, male-oriented work, which is not to judge the quality of the work, men's or women's—which ran from excellent to awful. It is just to comment again on what was acceptable and expected for a woman to write.

I know that now. I didn't then. I identified with the male poets—not realizing of course that to most of them I was a woman, no different than any other. Sex and romantic relationships had their place—usually after the important business of the day, and night. No matter how much I came later to love and at one point even be obsessed by Norma, I didn't want her anywhere near the poetry readings, and it wasn't just because I was hiding the fact I was gay. That was where I hung out with my friends, and no place for her.

Around that time, Allen Katzman and I went to a party at filmmaker Ron Rice's loft. Rice had just finished a new movie. (His movie "The Flower Thief" which starred Taylor

Mead was a Beat film classic.) It was a huge space, but everyone crowded into one large room to hear the entertainment for the evening. A newcomer named Tiny Tim—it might even have been his first performance—was going to sing, and sing he did, strumming his ukulele to "Tiptoe through the Tulips." His squeaky falsetto voice coming out of what seemed endless amounts of hair. A murmur went through the crowd as someone whispered that the famous Neil Cassidy was coming. A man strutted into the room wearing very tight white sailor pants. I don't know what I expected, but if that was Neil Cassidy, he didn't seem to me like the hero of Kerouac's *On the Road*. He just seemed rough and rather crude. Then, as if to accentuate Tiny Tim's last song, there was a loud shout, angry voices, and someone broke a chair over Rice's head. Within moments there was a free-for-all and Allen and I looked for the nearest exit. The fight was one thing, but the room reeked of marijuana and it was obvious it was only a matter of time before the police would arrive. It seemed a good time for us to leave.

The opposite of that performance was the now famous dance concert at the Judson Church where Robert Morris and Yvonne Rainer danced in slow motion, nude—albeit holding each other close, face to face. The evening opened with Yvonne Rainer dancing solo. The only other time I had ever seen a performer command so much attention by her very presence on the stage was the afternoon when I first saw Peggy Lee. My stepfather "packaged" the Colgate Comedy Hour—he booked the acts and put the show together. One week it starred Abbott and Costello, the next Dean Martin and Jerry Lewis. Once in a while I would go to the filming of the show to help provide the laugh track. I couldn't have been more than seven or eight years old, but to this day I remember the moment Peggy Lee walked onto the stage. She was dressed in a gauzy white dress and I felt like I was literally seeing an angel—the closest image my child's mind could conjure up. That's how strong a stage presence she had. I hardly thought of Yvonne Rainer as an angel, but her presence was just as powerful when she began to dance with slow perfectly controlled rhythm to the music of Eric Satie. It was mesmerizing.

Allen Katzman and I had become lovers soon after I moved to Manhattan, or more accurately we had become great friends who occasionally made love. I was still seeing Sylvia as well as Norma. It was a confusing time, but I didn't try to make sense of it. Truthfully, I had no conception *how* to make sense of it.

Allen's twin brother Don was also an active poet and publisher. Some people had difficulty telling them apart. Maybe it was because I got to know Allen so well, but I never saw them as being particularly similar. Allen Katzman was a tall man, awkward in a graceful kind of way, prematurely balding, intense but good-natured, with a slow, careful manner of speaking—as if each sentence had to be first carefully thought out before being delivered. Allen hated superfluous words. In one of the pictures I still have of him he has a beard, probably a necessary accoutrement to editing the *East Village Other* and the appropriate fashion for the mid and late Sixties. I remember him best being clean shaven and walking, not fast, but with such a long stride it was nearly impossible to keep up with him. Allen loved to reminisce about the years he was stationed at Fort Sill in the town of Lawton. He had become friends with his platoon sergeant, who was Native American, and had stayed with him on and off for a year and a half in Commanche, a community of Apache army sergeants and their families. He published a book of poems, *Commanche Cantos*, based on that experience.

Many nights after the readings, we would all go dancing at the Dom, a large club on St. Mark's Place around the corner from the Metro. We often danced until closing. One night I "twisted" the night away with Allen Ginsberg and Jerry

Allen Katzman. *The East Village Other*, June 1968, vol. 13, #39.
Photo: Walter Brendel.

Bloedow to the music of The Beatles and the much more funky uptown rhythms.

Allen Katzman knew about my relationship with Norma. He didn't like her. Maybe it was jealousy, maybe it was just that he was a dear friend and could sense that she wasn't. He knew that during a six-month period when Norma and I weren't seeing each other, she had begun a relationship with Jimmy, a mutual friend. Jimmy and Allen and I had worked together on a series of four chapbooks which we put out under the auspices of the Hardware Poets Playhouse and Hespiridian Press, Allen and Don's imprint.

Allen didn't tell me about Norma and Jimmy because he didn't want to hurt me, particularly after I began spending night after night sleeping in Norma's room in the hospital when I thought she was dying from a ruptured appendix and peritonitis. The night of her appendectomy, she had cried out my name in her delirium. The hospital called me and I spent all day at work and all night in the hospital for over a week, barely eating. The more I was with her, the more involved with her I became. She remained in the hospital for over a month. I moved in with her to take care of her when she returned home. I found out about her relationship with Jimmy two months later, when she was finally well enough to be on her own.

My apartment on Suffolk Street was broken into the same week I gave Norma an ultimatum, Jimmy or me, and since she refused to make a decision, walked out. I couldn't bear remaining in the mess the thieves had made of what was left of my few possessions. They had packed up almost everything I had in my suitcases—most of my clothes, a gold watch and some jewelry I had brought from home, and my prize possession, a small 16mm movie camera—and exited down the stairs, after first smearing the walls with ink. No doubt frustrated that their break-in wasn't worth the effort. There wasn't anything of real value—to them.

Seeing how upset I was about both the break-up and break-in, Allen urged me to move in with him temporarily until I could settle down and find another place. So I moved into his apartment on Ninth Street and Second Avenue.

A permanent state of temporary: A perfect description of how Allen Katzman lived. There were no pictures, very little furniture. The stove, the sink—nothing seemed used. Two years after he rented it, the apartment looked like he had just moved in. Neither of us ever shopped or cooked. We lived on take-out, sharing our favorite meal—a giant ham and cheese sandwich on thick, dark pumpernickel bread, smeared with plenty of hot mustard, from Zookies, a neighborhood deli.

In spite of all that, I enjoyed living with Allen and probably would have stayed longer if it wasn't for his persistent and very annoying habit of leaving his clothes wherever they happened to drop and not maintaining the apartment. I finally got it together and moved out after getting stuck in his tiny, windowless bathroom for over two hours while he fumbled with a lock I had begged him for almost a month to fix.

Paul Blackburn kindly shepherded me around the Lower East Side looking for a place after I decided to leave Allen's. One apartment we saw for $125 a month—a small fortune in those days—on the corner of Avenue C and 4th Street, had only cold running water, three empty beer bottles on what was left of the windowsill, and all the interior doors off their hinges, leaning precariously against their respective doorframes. Luckily, just as I was about to give way to despair, Paul learned that the poet Gilbert Sorrentino's apartment on Ninth Street between Avenues B and C was about to be vacated.

About six months later, an apartment became available in the building across the street above Carol Bergé who lived on the second floor of a small back building. The first floor was occupied by Alison, a painter, and her two children. The top floor had just been vacated. The entrance was an ironwork stairway that led up from a small courtyard. It was the whole floor, small, but with five rooms—a central room leading into a circular configuration of bathroom, kitchen, bedroom, living room and what became a storage room. Sixteen windows. I couldn't believe my luck.

Shortly after I moved, Norma and Jimmy announced their decision to get married. For some reason, I didn't hold a grudge and even went to their decidedly bizarre wedding in a huge Catholic church uptown. Built to hold hundreds, that day it was populated by their wedding party of about ten, most of whom one or the other or both had slept with.

A few years later Norma was killed in an automobile accident, and many years after that Allen was too. Although our lives had drifted apart well before that, Allen Katzman remains one of those people I will always think of and remember with gratitude and love.

THE HARDWARE POETS PLAYHOUSE

In January 1962, Jerry and Elaine Bloedow, along with Peter Dan Levin and his wife, Audrey Davis, founded the Hardware Poets Playhouse. It was located in a loft over a hardware store on West 54th Street and Sixth Avenue and came with a ready-made marquee *HARDWARE* in bright, bold letters.

Even when you entered in the evening, struggling up a long narrow flight of stairs, the theater glowed like mid-afternoon. The Hardware Poets Playhouse, instead of being dark like most small theaters and rehearsal spaces, was awash with light. Originally the loft had been painted black, but Jerry demanded we repaint it white to encourage authentic audience participation, not the usual forced scripted "spontaneity." In the light, the audience's reactions, gestures, even their whispered comments to each other, would became part of the action. It was obvious this was not going to be a theater where attention was focused only in one direction—face front.

The same sense of serious playfulness that had attracted me to Diane and La Monte in Berkeley initially drew me to the Hardware Poets Playhouse. A sense of fun and exploration due in no small part to Jerry, whose poems were a mixture of Gertrude Stein and Ignatz the Kat, with an underlying progressive politic antedating what many of us would later grow into.

Because he was an actor, co-founder Peter Dan Levin was primarily concerned with how actors work, how they understand their relationship to the script. Along with Jerry, Dan's wife Audrey was originally supposed to direct most of the plays. When Audrey decided against participating as a director, Dan took over. Jerry and Dan were a perfect artistic match. Jerry always seemed to be on his feet, in motion, talking, joking. Dan was much quieter, more introspective. Jerry put the difference best: "My interest was mostly in

101

the writing and the mechanics of theater. Dan was very interested, because of his training, in the inner life of the actor, of the character as assumed by an actor—the living presence of theater. To hell with all the hardware and all the fancy lighting and all the rest of the special effects. And he was very critical and stringent. He didn't want us to be self-indulgent and mushy and sentimental and soft-headed, and he was very strong about the actors having strong participation, not just mouthing lines. I would have been perfectly happy if people just recited my lines. But he taught us to care about the actors."

As a poet I understood how Jerry felt. I had never been involved in the production of a play before the Hardware Poets Playhouse, and I couldn't understand why the actors needed a personal history mapped out for them. Did Hamm and Clove in Beckett's *Endgame* have an underlying storyline? Except for their culinary connection, of course. Or Winnie and Willie in *Happy Days*? We don't know how they got where they are when the play opens, or why they are the way they are. Most of the mystery of the play lies in the fact that *they just are.* Because their place is anyplace, it could be where you are or I am. So, if I had a character Raymont, a scientist, practical and pragmatic, who makes paper airplanes and thinks he is superior to Gilmont, a dreamer who spends his days picking flowers out of the play's backdrop, to me they were just two characters who made paper airplanes and picked flowers out of a backdrop.

But trained actors, particularly Actors Studio actors, don't see things that way. Just like ordinary humans they need motivation; they need to know "why." Dan gave the characters in the plays of mine he directed a life beyond what I had written for them. He taught me how to write a satirical character, not just an empty caricature, and in the process, I, who had after all created the characters, began to better understand myself.

But with all that, the spirit of the Hardware Poets

Playhouse reflected more than anything else Jerry's uncanny inventiveness. All of us who were involved with the theater were encouraged to forget the "rules," to free our imagination, experiment—and have fun.

This was truly a poets' theater.

I spent several years working with the Hardware Poets Theater—from 1962 and its original loft location, to its second loft home, to its relocation to Good Shepherd-Faith Presbyterian and finally to La Mama ETC in 1966, when the last two plays I did under Hardware's auspices were performed.

Along with Jerry, I loved the Theater of the Absurd—my favorite playwright was Samuel Beckett, whose theatrical vision fit perfectly with two of my favorite books, Lewis Carroll's *Alice in Wonderland* and *Alice Through the Looking Glass.*

I disliked the Alice books as a child because I found the world of Wonderland to be bizarre and disturbing. Maybe it was too much like the world of my childhood. I rediscovered the books in of all places a graduate philosophy course. As an adult, I was able to fully appreciate Carroll's sense of humor and twists of logic.

"Mr. Samson, Eleanor & I" was my first venture into playwriting and, it turned out, directing for the theater. An experimental play in one act about two men and a woman who lived together in a rooming house, two of them *perhaps* imaginary, it opened for Jerry's epic work, "The Assault of Everest." Jerry's play incorporated many elements of vaudeville, and, as always, he encouraged audience participation. Both our plays incorporated elements of chance, a popular technique used by musicians like John Cage and poets like Jackson Mac Low, and echoed in ancient texts like the *I Ching*, where chance is seen as a vital element in understanding the exigencies of human existence.

Besides random elements, "Mr. Samson, Eleanor & I"

incorporated bits and pieces of various texts and, throughout one whole scene, Eleanor sat in a rocking chair eating watermelon—I liked the way watermelon smelled. At the last minute the actor who was originally supposed to play Mr. Samson threw down the script in frustration, shouting, "I can't do this" and walked out.

Dan knew Richard Mulligan (of future sit-com fame, first in "Soap" and then as Dr. Jerry Weston in "Empty Nest") from the Actors Studio and asked him to play the part. Dan and Jerry pitched in to help with the directing. Mulligan had hardly any rehearsal, and there was no time to learn the lines, so he figured out how to put the script at different parts of the stage so he could read it without anyone noticing. He gave a terrific performance.

Directing was hard—particularly as a woman many years younger than any of the actors—but I learned a great deal more than if I had just watched someone else. If I had followed my own stage directions, the characters would have walked on each other's heads, fallen off the stage, and wound up speaking with their backs to the audience. I also learned that one of the biggest differences between writing a play and writing poems is that one has to be much more direct when writing for the stage. Unless ideas are clearly delineated, they can be easily missed. The actors, their movements, the scenery are distracting. Because physicality and action were stressed in our theater company, I learned how to write plays where people moved and related to each other and didn't just speak lines at each other's heads.

With my first play, the theater literally became my home. Lacking resources, I had to bring most of what there was of my furniture, including my bed, to act as the set, and consequently I often slept there, exhausted from working all day and rehearsing long into the night. The stage was raised and carpeted to keep down the noise, which conveniently helped to further the illusion—both of stage and real bedroom. Opening night went well, but I spent it in the bathroom of the Chinese restaurant next to the Hardware Store racked with nerves and diarrhea. That evening, I never even saw the play.

Writing plays also allowed me to experiment with humor for the first time, and the pathos and sometimes sinister aspect underlying humor. I tried to refine the theme of "daily ritual" I had touched on in "Mr. Samson, Eleanor and I" in my next play "A Hatrack Named Georgie." Earl, the main character, lives in the center of a cornfield—no house, just a bed, dresser, a few pails of paint, and his hat rack. Each of his objects is painted a different color, each has its own name, and Earl has a specific ritual—a set of very rigid rules—to guide his every action.

Ritual, of course, presupposes sacrifice.

As the play opens, Earl has already sacrificed his plant because its name was also Earl—he found that too confusing. He has decorated his hat rack, Georgie, with bright red and purple and green ribbons and is chanting to it and presenting it with gifts, each one neatly packaged. During the course of the play, Earl is an amusing and eccentric character who gradually becomes more sinister and less amusing as the play progresses. We had the stage rigged so part of the audience would be closed off at the final curtain when, after sacrificing Georgie, Earl begins to draw a circle around "his" audience, chanting to them, presenting them with gifts, the colorful ribbons torn off Georgie—preparing to sacrifice the isolated audience members in their turn. One night the show went over so well one of the audience members actually screamed and threw himself on the floor.

The Hardware Poets Playhouse became my second home and Jerry and Elaine surrogate family. Elaine, in particular, was someone I trusted completely, who I could talk to and confide in, who I knew would tell me the truth, without prejudice or hidden agenda. I also had tremendous respect for Elaine's ability to manage the quite complex business of the theater at the same time she was taking care of her and

Scenes from the "Assault of Everest" by Jerry Bloedow, 1967.
Hardware Poets Theater. Back cover graphic from *The Assault of Everest* by
Jerry Bloedow, 1967.

Jerry's new baby, Beth. Besides how could I not have a high regard for someone who had read all forty of my Oz books? The Hardware Poets Playhouse also did a series of musical events, dramatic readings and poetry and open play readings. One of the biggest Hardware events was YAM day (May spelled backwards) which ran 60 hours. It was one of the first avant-garde festivals in New York. George Brecht and Elaine were the primary organizers. Hardware Poets also did evenings of mixed media—having live actors perform in front of film—long before the psychedelic years that would come later.

It was a running joke that the theater was so popular because we served gallons of jug wine during the intermission. If your play went on last, you were assured of an enthusiastic audience reaction.

Then along came the 1964 World's Fair and suddenly we started getting summons at the theater and at Le Metro where the readings were still running. One rumor was the city was trying to clean up its image for the massive influx of tourism expected for the fair. Another was that traditional theaters and venues, particularly in the West Village, were out to shut down any competition. The campaign against alternative art escalated. Finally, we banded together and succeeded in keeping the new off-off Broadway theaters and the poetry readings alive against the tide of repression. It was during this struggle that I met Ellen Stewart, the founder of La Mama ETC. She and her theater would become staunch allies, both politically and artistically.

It wasn't until I began running a bookstore, organizing readings, events, editing and publishing a magazine, and putting on plays myself that I could begin to understand, even if in a very small way, the work and dedication and financial sacrifice involved in Jerry and Elaine, Dan and Audrey's operating the Hardware Poets Playhouse.

Meanwhile, the readings at Le Metro lasted until 1965 when a combination of Moe and Cindy finally moving on, a series of conflicts with some of the poets—notably a group of African American poets including Calvin Hernton and David Henderson who published a magazine called *Umbra*— and the shifting of interest caused by the rising psychedelic culture in mixed-media performance and rock and roll led to the cafe being closed.

After I was fired from the Daniel Mead Literary Agency, I went on unemployment insurance. Around that time Bob Nichols introduced me to Grace Paley. At that point I hadn't read Grace's work, but unlike many writers whose personalities seem so different from their words, the humor and warmth of her stories was an accurate reflection of her personality. For me, reading her work later was hearing and seeing Grace all over again. Bob and Grace hired me to mind the office and sell peace buttons at the Greenwich Village Peace Center. Mary Perot Nichols, Bob's wife at the time, was an editor at the *Village Voice*. She got me a part-time job typing *Voice* classified ads two days a week for $28. Between the two jobs I managed since my rent was only $40 a month.

That was when the *Voice* was sixteen pages long—before the newspaper strike that put the paper, with its "Apartments for Rent" section, on the map. The term "the East Village" was actually coined by Rose Ryan, who was then head of the *Voice Classified*, at the behest of rental agents who wanted a more glamorous title to help rent apartments in that part of the Lower East Side which was the eastern extension of Greenwich Village. For a while, I became the *Voice* poetry editor on the side and wrote book reviews and one summer wrote theater reviews to fill in while *Voice* critic Michael Smith was on vacation.

With whatever else happened to me during those years, I was extraordinarily lucky in my friendships. Without Diane's I never would have met the poets or become involved in the world of poetry in New York. Allen Katzman and Theodore Enslin, Robert Nichols, Grace Paley, Jerry and Elaine Bloedow—I can't imagine those years without them. And so many others: Carol Bergé, Jerry Rothenberg and Robert Kelly. The Deux Megots, the Metro, The Hardware Poets Playhouse were home to me. They were and remain a living memory to which, above all else, I return as one returns home—for sustenance, renewal, continuity, support.

KELLI'S CASTLE

I remember clearly the first time I saw Kelli. It was at the home of a friend. I have forgotten his name even though he was the one who introduced me to her. His father had left him an extremely lucrative business in New Jersey renting jukeboxes and cigarette machines to bars and clubs. He certainly wasn't the stereotypical "mob" figure conjured up by cigarette and jukebox concessions, although those connections might have been there. He was probably in his early thirties, rather clean-cut in a preppie kind of way, knew quite a bit about art and literature, had very good taste in both, and adored Kelli.

Stepping into the large rectangular living room of his Greenwich Village townhouse, all I could focus on was a singularly attractive young woman bent backwards almost to the floor who was playing a game popular at the time involving two people holding a string taut while the others attempted to pass underneath—each successful round bringing the string lower until one by one the group was weeded out.

There, commanding the center of attention, was Kelli, literally dancing her way to victory.

Slightly athletic by the standards of the Sixties, lithe, with striking green eyes, Kelli was the kind of woman everyone was drawn to immediately, men and women alike. She was that variety of charming extrovert whose photo you could easily envision over the title "Most Popular" in the high-school yearbook, the cheerleader of the Fifties—not the semi-soft-core acrobat of today, but the girl-next-door type with a pony tail and endless energy who could inspire your team to any act of prowess.

At least, I was to find out later, when she was high.

Kelli tended bar at Slugs, a jazz club and drug hangout on Fourth Street between Avenues B and C which would gain notoriety both for the excellence of its musicians—Joe Henderson, Archie Shep, Hank Mobley, Kenny Durham among them—and the seediness of its atmosphere. It was finally closed in the 70s after trumpet player Lee Morgan was shot to death on the stage by his common-law wife. Slugs provided the perfect foil for Kelli, making her fresh scrubbed demeanor all the more alluring. Even I was taken in by it until one night, while waiting for her to close the bar, I saw her blithely pick up two full cases of beer that would have been difficult for a man to lift.

Slugs was also a place where it was easy for a good-looking, personable bartender to get free samples amid a flourishing heroin trade. Unfortunately, finding out Kelli was a junkie only made her a more romantic figure in my ingenuous post-Beat Generation eyes. She didn't use needles, which would have been a turnoff even to my impressionable young mind, but slowly and deliberately inhaled the sticky white powder from one well-manicured fingertip.

Besides which Kelli represented all the qualities I felt I lacked, which is not unusual in someone you find that appealing. She seemed to be in complete control of every situation, without the abrasiveness that sometimes goes along with extreme self-confidence. She was the ultimate seductress. Even when I knew better, the attraction remained—if a bit tarnished. When the time came to move on, my reaction was one of bewilderment rather than torment. I had by this time seen quite a bit of the underside of Kelli's considerable charm.

Our relationship lasted exactly one month, almost to the day.

The problems began when it became obvious that after trying heroin a couple of times it didn't appeal to me at all.

Lying rigid on the bed, my body stretched taut, I felt trapped, physically restrained. A short while before I had drunk some of the orange soda Kelli had advised, laughing, that junkies drink to make the almost inevitable throwing up easier. But it didn't make it easier for me. I didn't want to throw up. I didn't want to lie there, motionless, to avoid it. Nothing was happening. No new sights, sounds. Even the hysteria of my experience with psilocybin was preferable to this void, this numbness of body and spirit. Heroin— this pain killer I had taken almost two hours before that refused to wear off.

I stared numbly around the room, only my eyes moving. I was in a downstairs bedroom, facing a blank TV. I wished desperately it was on. Anything to make time pass. The walls of the bedroom were that faded white color that could be yellow or tan or gray depending on the light. A small lamp, one of those shiny green or blue animal shapes you buy in the dime store, offered the only real illumination. Unlike the rest of the house, which was carefully decorated in 14th Street bargain-basement splendor, this room looked barren, like the inside of an empty refrigerator. There was something not quite right about it. It was a room that had somehow been missed.

Kelli said she had to go out: "I'll be back later."

"How much later?" Anxiety rose in my throat, a palpable thing, threatening to choke me. I had to go to the bathroom, knew it was futile. Even if I could manage to get myself up without getting sick, it would take hours before my body would respond.

Heroin is a drug that is supposed to make you easy, erase fear. I could hardly remember ever feeling so anxious. If there is one thing I can't stand, that supersedes all else, it is the inability to move, if necessary, to run. That is what terror means to me.

Being held, unwillingly, in place.

Kelli lived in a small building on the Upper West Side that looked like a miniature fortress. Kelli's Castle, her friends called it. She occupied the upper two floors as well as a small attic-like room that resembled a turret, leading from the second floor. One could easily picture a flag gracefully balanced on the pointed rooftop, swaying in the summer breeze, its emblem visible for miles around. A vivid contrast to the notorious single room occupancy hotel directly across the street.

Exactly one week after we met, Kelli announced dramatically as we walked down Broadway, my hand squeezed firmly in hers, that she thought it very likely she was in love.

We never had a chance.

We had made love twice before, both times at my apartment. This was the first time I had been to her home. As soon as we entered her apartment, she switched the light on and immediately went to the downstairs bathroom and began running a bath, calling to me to follow her.

Her bathroom looked like something out of a Sunday-supplement ad. Everything was pink. The bathtub, toilet, sink were pink enamel. The walls were painted pink. The floor was covered in pink tile. There were pink stuffed animals on a glass shelf over the sink, surrounded by seashell dishes holding tiny bars of pink soap.

Telling me to undress and she had a special treat for me, her voice took on an undertone of command that I was happy enough to obey. I began to undress very slowly, just in case she might change her mind, or I might decide to leave— which was not likely.

I finally stood naked, nervous and embarrassed, as she knelt beside the tub still fully dressed, steam now rising softly around the newly formed bubbles.

Getting up, she guided me to the tub and gently began sponging me with a thick soft pink cloth, as she whispered to me to relax. Her touch was reassuring. Her voice was so soothing, I almost forgot where I was and began to drift into sleep—the sound of her voice, the sweet smell of the bubbles blending together in a melodic fragrance.

I was almost unconscious by the time she urged me up on my feet, wrapping me in a huge pink bath towel. Putting her arm solicitously around my shoulder, she led me upstairs to her king-sized bed, where she carefully took the towel from around me and, folding it neatly, put it on a large overstuffed chair.

I sat on the bed watching her, fully awake now, as she undressed, unhurried, as if she had all the time in the world. She took off each piece of clothing and, folding it, put it carefully on the chair. When she was done, she sat down beside me and took me in her arms with the same deliberate ease. For a second the thought crossed my mind that maybe she was planning to fold me up too and place me on top of the pile of clothes that lay so neatly beside us.

And so began a virtuoso performance by a virtuosic performer. Positioning me on the bed—her bedroom, unlike the bathroom, was almost entirely free of any decoration—she lay on top of me in such a way that our bodies, our sex, fit together seamlessly as she began to move her hands slowly and sensuously over my body, missing nothing, as she kissed my eyes, my neck, the sides of my face, drawing me closer and closer into her, until I was so full of her I could hardly breathe.

Our orgasm when it came was rich and deep, but it was not to end there. We had barely rested for five minutes, when she turned slowly on her back and drew me on top of her, and we began again—without words or any other kind of distraction, with only the delight in our own arms and hands and mouths and bodies.

With only our delight in being women, being together.

All through that night and into the next morning, hardly pausing, we made love, as Kelli taught me how to receive and give love to another woman. Without guilt, without ambiguity, without reservation.

If I had thought about it, it might have occurred to me that no one could be that good a lover and teacher without a whole lot of practice, but at the time I wasn't doing much thinking. Night after night I came back to her, anticipating a repetition of that extravagant night. We never made love like that again. The artist had exhausted both her repertoire of tricks and the energy it took to perform them.

I look down now at a small photograph of myself naked, but discreetly posed, looking very pensive and very vulnerable, that Kelli had persuaded me would make her happy, and wonder at how much wider a place the world seemed then— filled with so many endless possibilities, unknown adventures. Or maybe it was just that it was a time before the past began to cast forth its own expectations, making the unknown far more desirable than any repetition of past delights.

When she wasn't high, Kelli was very quiet, complained a lot, and could be downright unpleasant. One evening she admitted that when she wasn't on drugs she was so sensitive to pain even her shirt touching the back of her neck hurt her unbearably. Much to my horror, I began to realize that often when it came time to see her, I would be hoping half-heartedly that she was high.

Kelli did do one very important thing for me. Because she was so uninhibited she tore down, at least temporarily, my own inhibitions. She loved to be affectionate in public, neck in art galleries, on the street. The reverse side was that Kelli needed desperately to be the center of attention, to be unique. She needed to be the one white woman in a group of black women—she frequented the Harlem gay bars—or the one woman in a group of men, gay or straight.

I saw Kelli several times after we stopped being lovers. Actually she had begun seeing someone else shortly after her declaration of love. She was very up front about it, told me not to pay any attention, she was just like that, loved to party, have fun. One night she met a eighteen-year-old African American woman named Randy, who was very small, very butch, and very sweet—really a kid. Soon after that Kelli told me that Randy was going to move in with her.

It is no secret that addicts are users. For someone who is so dependent on a substance over which they have no control, they need to feel in total control of every other aspect of their lives.

About six months after she and Randy started living together, Kelli invited me over to her house to meet some friends from Latin America who were in New York for the weekend. After a good dinner and a couple of hours of talk, they left and she encouraged me to stay a while longer.

I still found Kelli extremely attractive and although any strong feelings I'd had for her had passed, a residue of that old longing remained. Kelli beckoned me to a chair, urged me to sit down, relax, have another cup of coffee while she and Randy cleaned up. "No, we don't need your help, you'll just get in the way. Would you like to hear some music?"

She turned on the radio, humming softly in rhythm to the music. Then, suddenly, but slowly—if you can imagine the combination of the two—she threw her towel down on the counter and began to dance provocatively. Taking Randy in her arms, she continued dancing, more slowly and more provocatively, while I sat there watching, cup in hand.

I decided it was definitely time to leave, but Kelli urged me to stay a few more minutes and keep Randy company— she had to run down to the store for cigarettes and more coffee for the morning. She was out the door before I could say anything, and the next thing I knew Randy was coaxing me into the downstairs bedroom, which didn't take much coaxing at that point, although it was Kelli I really wanted to be with.

After about twenty minutes of perfunctory love-making,

Kelli reappeared, noisily ringing the outside bell so we could let her in. The excuse once she got inside was that she had forgotten her key. She looked rather pleased with herself. I beat a hasty retreat. This time it was not disputed.

It was obviously a set-up, but whether it was for my amusement, or for Randy's, or like everything else, for Kelli herself, I have no idea. At the time I imagined our little interlude being an appetizer for the main event that would take place when I left. Now I suspect there was little sensual about it, that my first impulse to consider it just another one of Kelli's sexual turn-ons was wrong. I suspect both Randy and I were only unpaid, if not unwilling, actors in a scene whose final meaning we could not begin to comprehend since it resided firmly in Kelli's head, heart, and past. That ultimately she was the only one who derived any real pleasure from it, seeing a well plotted scheme, cleverly staged, work out exactly according to plan, for her most demanding audience, herself.

I didn't see Kelli much after that. After a while, I learned that she had entered a drug rehabilitation program with Randy, who was treated very badly by the hospital staff who blamed her, as a black woman, for Kelli's addiction, although the exact opposite was true.

Several years went by when I again met the friend who had first introduced us and found out that the last time he had heard of Kelli she was in a very bad way, was on drugs again, had run out of money, been beaten up—her jaw wired together—and was living with some man she knew from her days at Slugs.

I went by her apartment to see if there was anything I could do, but her name was no longer on the bell and no one who was there could tell me what had happened to her or where she had gone.

No one taught me more in those early years in New York about the juncture of image and reality than Kelli. To this day I never pass that street on the Upper West Side without thinking of her and wondering if she is still alive, hoping she is still around somewhere, having bounced back once again as she was wont to do, finally happy, at last, in one of her imagined games.

THE DEATH OF A FRIEND

Colors shot from the ceiling. Straight and sharp. So thick you could hold them. I was drifting in time. The only sound was a faint, monotonous hum. Gold showered from the walls. It's just like Baudelaire, I thought, and laughed.

The radio sounded like Donald Duck. Stop, I directed with my finger. And it stopped. Everything became perfectly motionless. Everything that was "real." I rose into the silence, my head inches from the ceiling. Alison swore she saw me disappear.

It was hours later when we first touched. We didn't mean to. It certainly wasn't planned. We were exhausted and lay down, together, to sleep. And there it was between us, thick and impenetrable. A feeling dense as fear.

Finally, perhaps, it is an accumulation of small things that changes us, the unexpected and unnoticed incidents that signal moments of transition, pointing us in an entirely different direction, almost without our knowledge, often without our consent.

November 17, 1965. Rush hour. The bus was crowded. An old woman, pale, sat across the aisle from me, years hanging from her hands. I could see the street between elbows and knees. A man coughed, lunged forward. No one moved. No one *could* move. There was a buzzing in my ears; my mouth tasted funny. I felt tired, confused, a little sick. But it was bright out. The street, what I could see of it, looked clean and clear. It was hard to be worried on such a morning. I looked at Alison. She smiled, laughed, took my hand.

Noon. We were still waiting, had been waiting for hours. In a basement, poor, cramped. How much all institutional rooms have in common. How easily one could be substituted for another. We were in family court, but we could be in a criminal courtroom, a Medicaid office, Welfare, the unemployment office, a hospital ward, a schoolroom in the Bronx or Brooklyn or Queens. All painted green. Serviceable green. Soothing green. Ugly, dull, depressing green.

Designed to keep you quiet, hypnotize you, make you incapable of thought, motion, speech.

A guard brought us coffee.

"Do you have a lawyer?"

"No."

"That's good."

"Good?"

"Sure."

"Why? I don't understand. I was thinking of asking for a postponement until I could get a lawyer."

"Look, this judge is a nice guy. He'll feel more sympathetic toward you if you go in there and look to him for protection. He's very protective of mothers. A lawyer would just put him off."

Helpful. Solicitous. Persuasive. "You're much better off this way, believe me. I've been here for fifteen years now, I know. This man doesn't believe children should be separated from their mother. He'll never take the kids away from you unless he gets mad for some reason. That's why it's better to appeal to him."

He gently nudged her arm. "You know what I mean."

Turning to me. "Who are you?"

"I'm her friend. I came to testify for her."

"Do you want some more coffee? It could be a long time."

"Yes, some more coffee. Please."

Trust is, for some people, an automatic response. It is not in their nature to be suspicious of people. This was a trait Alison and I shared. We had met the year before when Alison, an artist and my downstairs neighbor, had volunteered to paint the sets for a play I had written and was directing at the Hardware Poets Playhouse. We had been friends for six months when a mutual friend who was a doctor working with R. D. Laing turned us on to some hospital grade LSD he had brought with him from London. Unlike the experience I'd

had with psilocybin at Berkeley, I didn't have any psychological revelations with LSD. The experience was intense,
but it lasted too long. I never had any desire to take it again.
For Alison, LSD became a source of inspiration. She loved
the bright primary colors and visual distortions which now
permeated her work.

I had gotten tired of rats in the kitchen and footsteps on
the roof, of staying up all night protecting a kitten I had gotten
to protect me and had finally moved from my Ninth Street
apartment, but I came back on a distress call from Alison
telling me her parents were threatening to take her children
away from her and she had to go to court and would I come.

"But, Alison, how could you possibly think that by
swallowing paint it would come out of your fingertips and
you could avoid using a brush?"

"It was a beautiful idea, wasn't it? I wanted to be close to
the canvas, to touch it, to feel the color pouring out of me. I
wanted to paint the sun."

Two o'clock. Four cups of coffee. The same room. Endless
cigarettes. Should she call a lawyer, postpone the case? Could
it even be postponed?

"What could they have against me? What did I do? What
should I do?"

"Look, it can't hurt to postpone the case. Get some better
advice. Get more people together."

"But I want it over with. And maybe this guy is right. He
seems nice enough, and, after all, who would know better
than him. You heard what he said—they never take children
from their mother. How much longer will it take? How much
longer will they make us wait?"

"Alison. Listen."

"Look, it's all right. My parents are a little crazy. They
want to worry me, keep me in line. They object to my being
a painter, my black boyfriend. They have no proof of
anything. They're only trying to scare me. They've been after

me for years. But basically they love me. They wouldn't do anything to really hurt me."

"Alison..."

"Don't worry. I'm not worried. Everything will be all right. I'll just tell the judge how much I love my kids. You'll tell him." Smiling. "How could anyone not believe you, not trust you to tell the truth. Don't worry. I'll cooperate. I'll do anything they say. Everything will be fine."

They said she might have won finally, maybe even at the next hearing, if—on being told her children would be "temporarily" taken away—she hadn't tried to attack the judge. I was never called. It was a foregone conclusion, a trap.

After that Alison was never the same. They committed her to Bellevue for observation, and when I visited her, her eyes were glassy with sorrow and drugs. She was let out ten days later only to be picked up again within the month, dragged screaming off the street by the police. Her parents came to collect her things. Her children were living with them, going to a private school in Colorado, learning the proper way to behave.

There is one painting of hers I still have. A painting of the sun. An orange sun, its rays thick and impenetrable, sharp and straight.

A RIOT, A MAGAZINE, A "MARRIAGE"

On November 22, 1963, John F. Kennedy was assassinated in Dallas and Lyndon Johnson was sworn in as president. I had voted for Kennedy. Not because I was particularly taken with him but because, like most Californians I knew, I was appalled by how Nixon had red-baited Helen Gahagan Douglas to win his Senate seat. Even though Johnson supported the Civil Rights Bill which passed Congress in the spring of 1964, that summer New York and New Jersey were rocked by riots—a foreshadowing of the uprising in Watts that would erupt on August 11, 1965.

So far there had been no trouble on our block or in our immediate neighborhood, a community comprising a mixture of races and ethnicities who generally got along quite well. There was nowhere near the homeless population that followed Mayor Ed Koch's emptying of the mentally ill out of state hospitals onto the streets and mushroomed during the Reagan presidency when funds were cut from public housing projects. Apart from the Bowery, you rarely saw anyone begging on the streets, but some of the blocks, particularly those south of Sixth Street and east of Avenue B, sported an active drug trade; theft was common, and many of the tenement buildings were badly maintained and overcrowded.

It wasn't advisable for a woman to be out alone late at night in our neighborhood, although I often was. One night, crossing Tompkins Square Park around eleven o'clock, I was surrounded by a gang of teenagers who taunted me and threw bottles at me, one breaking across my ankle. I looked so frightened one of the boys took pity on me and told the others to leave me alone. Besides that one incident in the park, I never had any trouble.

Until the summer of '63.

The heat seemed exaggerated, as if some malignant forces were conspiring to make things as unpleasant and uncomfortable as possible. Even the streets seemed dirtier than usual—not that the blocks east of Avenue A were ever particularly well-tended. The heat went on day after relentless day until everyone was on edge. The Ukrainian woman who owned the grocery store down the street, usually full of humor and gossip, barely spoke as she sliced my weekly ration of bread and packaged the cheese and hot dogs that would serve as my evening meal.

One evening a brick was thrown through the window of a black family's apartment and it was rumored that the firebombing of an apartment building inhabited mostly by Puerto Ricans was a direct response. No one was hurt, but the tension became palpable.

There was a growing antagonism between members of the black and Puerto Rican communities, exacerbated by unemployment and inadequate housing. At the time, some African Americans felt that Puerto Ricans were reaping the gains they had struggled for, and some members of the Puerto Rican community wanted to be seen as white and resented African Americans. It is no revelation that without political awareness, groups—and individuals, for that matter—who are frustrated and live in close proximity turn on each other. A situation often aggravated by the authorities and the press.

I would recall the dynamics of that summer when I began to concretely experience the importance and powerful impact of ideologies that encourage both autonomy and coalition.

Two weeks later I experienced firsthand how a police force supposedly meant to quell trouble can in fact precipitate it.

I was walking from my apartment on Ninth Street east to Avenue C intending to pick up a newspaper before I caught the crosstown bus at Tenth Street to go to work. It was quite early and the streets were almost deserted. Suddenly a pistol shot rang out. I thought it was a car backfiring, so I didn't pay any attention and kept on walking. Within moments, the sound of police sirens blasted the empty streets, and dozens of police jumped out of their cars and lined Avenue C between Ninth and Tenth Streets, standing almost shoulder to shoulder, backs to the street and their patrol cars. Almost as one they drew their guns, and stood there, guns in hand, facing the empty sidewalks, facing the ground-floor windows of the tenements.

As if on cue, people began to emerge from apartments, stores, coffee shops, yelling and shoving, drawn to the scene by the police presence as more police poured into the area. I was frantic. I was almost at the bus stop and the bus was coming, but I could see through the front window the bus driver's panicked face. He looked like he had absolutely no intention of stopping. I shoved my way up the block and stood in the middle of Tenth Street waving my arms. Forced to at least slow down if he wasn't going to hit me, the driver opened the door, the bus still moving, and stopped for one brief instant as I literally jumped onto the bus, and it sped away.

Later I learned that the crowd had milled around for a while and finally drifted away when the news circulated that the gun shot had been the result of a domestic squabble. It was an eloquent lesson in how the police could provoke a community to riot.

At the time I was teaching at the Free University of New York—or the Free School as it later came to be called. The Free School was my first exposure to radical politics. I had joined the faculty because my friend Joe Burke had told methat Alan Krebs, who had been fired from his university position for traveling to Cuba, was starting an experimental school, and I could teach anything I wanted and get $400 a course. It sounded like a great opportunity, so I enthusi-astically prepared a course only to learn at the first faculty meeting that, not only was I *not* going to get $400, they were asking the organizing members of the school, including the faculty, to *contribute* money to get things going. At that point I couldn't back out.

So my teaching career began, at the Free School, for free.

In 1965, Nancy moved into my life. I had never really thought about living with anyone, and actually hadn't seen Nancy for almost a year when she arrived at my door on Ninth Street, suitcase in hand, announcing she had left the woman she had been living with. She settled in rapidly, attacking first my "storage room"—the extra room that was stacked with odds and ends from clothes to books to papers I didn't know where else to put. The next thing I knew she had packed me up just as neatly and transported me away from the East Village to a tidy one bedroom apartment on the Upper West Side.

I was ready to move. Norma was married and my relationship with Alison had soured. I was tired of noise and drugs and chaos and heat and tension. So when Nancy suggested moving to the newly-renovated apartment a friend's brother had just vacated, I happily agreed. I wanted to live with a woman. I wanted to be open about it. I was tired of living from one day to the next, never quite knowing what I was doing, where I was going, or who—if anyone—I was going there with.

I hated West Seventieth Street.

I don't like elevators and liked even less living on the eleventh floor of an elevator building in a block of elevator buildings. I felt isolated from my friends in the East Village. It didn't take me long to realize I had made a mistake. At one point I even deliberately provoked a fight so I would have an excuse to walk out and take the nearest subway home.

Except I no longer had a home.

Living uptown did give me time to finish my master's thesis. I had decided two years before to get my master's degree in philosophy. I had no intention of teaching at the time. I just wanted to take classes, and Hunter College was only $15 a credit, so even on my salary I could afford to take two classes a semester. Since I was still working on the *Voice Classified* I found a great deal on an apartment on Sixth Street and Second Avenue and made enough fuss so we finally moved back downtown—Nancy reluctantly, me enthusiastic about our large new space, even though it was rented "as is" and had more plaster on the floor than on the walls.

Arthur Sainer, a playwright and theater critic on the *Village Voice*, who had reviewed my first play and was familiar with my *Voice* reviews, asked me to review books and plays for a new magazine he was starting. He also invited me to be in on the planning meetings. That started the process that was to culminate in my becoming co-founder and editor of *IKON* magazine.

Both Arthur and I, even though we wrote theater reviews, were primarily writers and playwrights, not critics. We both felt art criticism was continually being used not only to *interpret* and *critique* art, literature, music, theater, but to *define* what constitutes art—limiting, if not altogether eliminating, both the artists' and audiences' input. Some critics saw themselves as the final arbiters, not only of taste, but of what art is. Postmodernist criticism often goes even further, defining not only what art is, but often defining into being the world that art inhabits, how we "the subjects" constitute our world and ourselves.

It was 1967 and "we"—the artists, writers, dancers, musicians, performers—were being told we couldn't write about the work of people we knew because we couldn't be objective. And we disagreed. We were being told that those who were deeply committed to a relationship, an artwork, a social cause, couldn't be objective. And we disagreed. We were told, even by sympathetic thinkers like Carl Jung, that the artist was too sensitive to deal with critical analysis, that our work came from the unconscious, and we were in no position to "understand" it.

And we disagreed.

After all, who is more capable of understanding the artistic process than the artist—to examine it, explain it, come to terms with it. "...working on the premise than the distinction between method and examination, between thought and fact is arbitrary and deadly."

Little did I realize then how prophetic the concluding words of that introductory editorial in the first issue of our new magazine *IKON* would turn out to be:

> ...information can serve as an impetus to action, not divorced from, but irrevocably a part of our involvement in this world, this present moment in which we find ourselves as participator and participant, our stance directed toward the future, not the past.

After almost a year of meetings, when it looked like *IKON* was no further toward being published than it had been during the first meeting, I said I would make sure the magazine got out, but only if I were the editor. If I was going to do the work, I wanted the decision-making power.

IKON would not have been possible without Nancy, who created sample covers, put the art staff together, and supported my decision. Arthur and his friend Thomas Muth, who put up the money for the first two issues, agreed, and after going through a large assortment of names we decided on IKON, spelled with a K to differentiate it from *icon* which was too connected with the religious symbolism of Russian religious icons. And also, not incidentally, looked better graphically. This was before *icon* reentered our vocabulary as a part of computer lingo.

We defined the word IKON to mean "an image combining symbolic elements into a unity in which all elements are perceived simultaneously thereby eliminating the separation of body and mind, spirit and intellect, feeling and thought."

IKON magazine, the first issue. February, 1967
Cover artwork by Stanley Sourelis

Angry Arts for Life and Against the War
Photos: Karl Bissinger

The first issue of *IKON* finally came out in February, 1967. It cost forty cents, had newstand distribution, and cost us about $1500 to print the initial 5000 copies. There were no grants available at the time. The magazine was totally financed by sales, subscriptions, what little advertising we had, and by our own salaries.

We stayed true to the spirit of our editorial. We printed an essay by Yvonne Rainer about her friend, the dancer Deborah Hay. Harold Herbstman, an actor and director, wrote about the Pagent Players; Arthur Sainer wrote about film and theater. Theodore Enslin wrote about Konrad Lorenz. There were poems by Robert Nichols and Anselm Hollo, short stories by Fielding Dawson, and Karl Bissinger's photos of Colette and Saul Steinberg. We ran a dialogue between Steve Paxton, a dancer, and Robby Robinson, an engineer, on "9 Evenings: Theater & Engineering" which had caused almost as much a sensation at the Armory as the Surrealist art show decades before. And Margaret Randall and Sergio Mondragon wrote to us about what was happening in Mexico.

Between February and July 1967, we published three issues of *IKON* and during that time both my life and the contents of the magazine began to change radically. By the third issue, Huey Newton and Bobby Seale had started the Black Panther Party in Oakland, Haight Ashbury was in full swing, draft resistance was gaining strength. In the five months between that February and July, in New York alone 10,000 people took part in the first Be-In in Central Park, and 400,000 marched against the war from Central Park to the UN. It was like being on a train out of control, the outside world flying by so fast it could only be perceived as splintered—each image more powerful than the last.

The war in Vietnam had begun to escalate along with the anti-war movement. Consequently, almost every story, poem, article in *IKON* 3 in one way or another related to the conflict. From Grace Paley's short story "The Sad Story About the Six Boys About To Be Drafted in Brooklyn" to Robert

Nichols's "Vietnam Journal," to Jean-Paul Sartre's Inaugural Address delivered at the Bertrand Russell War Crimes Tribunal in which he proclaimed that no matter what decision the judges in this "trial" decided "...the judges are everywhere; they are the peoples of the world, and in particular the American people." In "O and Ourselves," Allen Krebs stated quite succinctly that "political vocabularies" are not enough to "convey even a skeletal outline of the passion involved" in an exploitative society in which "sex equals cruelty, (and) power equals debasement."

Margaret Randall wrote about the eighth anniversary of the Cuban Revolution, and we ran a report on Angry Arts Against the War which had started out of a small meeting in the Greenwich Village Peace Center and evolved to a week in which over 500 artists presented forty events to almost 65,000 people. Once the week was over, the name was changed to Angry Arts *for Life* and Against the War—to promote a more positive image—and the poetry readings, concerts, exhibitions continued.

These were not just pieces in a magazine. Each represented an activity in which we were either directly or indirectly engaged. The magazine was beginning to fulfill its initial intent in a way I had certainly never conceived of. Sometimes I felt like a kind of Pygmalion, except I had helped to bring to life a magazine, not a person, and now *I* was under *its* spell.

My personal life? I ceased to have a personal life. As frantic as things were, it was only beginning. My relationship with Nancy was held together by the activities we did together, or was torn apart by them—who now can say which? The political community we were entering, mirroring the rest of society, was homophobic. Partly because, like the poetry world, the Left was dominated by heterosexual men, partly because homosexuality was seen by the orthodox Marxism of the time as bourgeois decadence, a diagnosis it paradoxically shared at the time with bourgeois moralists.

There was no support for our relationship, emotionally or intellectually. There was nowhere we could turn for help or advice, and even worse, we didn't recognize that anything could be different. Our relationship was without definition, outline, structure. We were held together by circumstance, and it would be circumstance that would finally tear us apart.

THE DIALECTICS OF LIBERATION

The Roundhouse on Chalk Farm Road in Camden Town, England, was a large, circular, barren building. First used as a railway terminal, it had been converted into an experimental theater and center for the arts by Arnold Wesker. Empty, it had a decimated look, contrasting sharply with the green suburban atmosphere of the bordering neighborhoods. In spite of its vastness, the Roundhouse generated a feeling of intimacy when more than three hundred and, during some events, up to three thousand people from all over the world gathered for two weeks beginning July 15, 1967, to participate in "The Dialectics of Liberation," a congress organized by the Institute for Phenomenological Studies in London. "The Dialectics of Liberation" was in every sense a congress in motion. Sometimes invigorating, often confusing, at times depressing, but always filled with energy—a microcosm of ideas and theories, a hodgepodge of messianic leaders and followers, a gathering of individuals and of groups, condensed into one space, for one short period of time.

The Dialectics of Liberation was the first conference of this nature I attended and was an apt precursor to the Cultural Congress of Havana I would participate in little more than a year later. On arriving in London from New York, I had the disorienting sensation of being transported into a time just slightly in the past—not fifty or one hundred years, more like four or five. The feeling was both comforting and deceptive. I was met by Joseph Berke, a psychiatrist and old friend from the Free School days, who had arranged for my invitation. He was now working with R. D. Laing, the psychiatrist who had gained notoriety because of his unorthodox view of psychosis. In two of his best-known books—*The Divided Self* and *The Politics of Experience and The Bird of Paradise*—Laing postulated that madness was a journey through which the distressed person must be guided, not an isolated unintelligible state. Laing also stressed the importance of the community and the family as causal factors.

Joe had originally come up with the idea of the conference and had worked two years on it as a part of the organizing committee which also included Laing, David Cooper, and Leon Redler. Since the congress wouldn't start for a few days, I took advantage of the time to see a little of London. I was staying with a couple who lived in one of the small enclaves that ringed the central part of the city. To my surprise, it never rained the whole month I was there. Every day was warm and sunny—much nicer than the hot, humid days I had left behind in New York.

When the Congress finally began, there was little time to do anything but attend the sessions and the events and discussions that accompanied them. In the morning were the public lectures, given by Gregory Bateson, Stokely Carmichael, David Cooper, John Gerrassi, Paul Goodman, Jules Henry, R. D. Laing, Herbert Marcuse, Ross Speck, and Paul Sweezy. In the afternoons, there were seminars and discussion groups limited to the participants, and in the evening sessions, which included a reading of Vietnamese poetry by the Buddhist monk, Thich Nhat Hanh, a program of Cuban poetry and films, a film on the dangers of technology by Roy Battersby, poetry readings, and a happening by Carolee Schneeman. The Provos were there from Holland. There were representatives from the Third World, students from West Berlin, and political activists from Norway and Sweden. There were representatives from the West Indies, Africa, Canada, America, Holland, Nigeria. Julian Beck arrived unexpectedly one afternoon to talk about the Living Theater. Allen Ginsberg chanted mantras and read poetry. Emmett Grogan talked about San Francisco and the Diggers. Everybody had ideas and opinions. Everybody talked. Sometimes there were just too many voices to hear anything at all.

With so much richness and variety of subject matter—from the social grouping of families, technology, schizophrenia, to communal living, political activism, economics, philosophy—it was impossible to do more than introduce topics, suggest areas of study and action. It wasn't so much what the speakers said. Anyone familiar with their work (which many at the conference weren't) would have been better off, in terms of any real analysis of their ideas, to read their books or to wait for a quieter moment to examine the contents of the lectures and discussions. The most interesting part of the conference came in the confrontation between the speakers, the organizers, the rest of the participants.

The point was that anybody could raise questions, make statements. There was widespread agreement and disagreement, both about the issues raised and the very structure of the conference itself. The crowd was at the same time willful and malleable, a crowd of followers as well as of individuals. Everyone agreed that a new unity of thought and feeling was replacing the sense of fragmentation and frustration typical of American society, that confrontation on the subject of violence was necessary not only for survival but to get at the deepest roots of the human dilemma.

There agreement ended.

R.D. Laing, in his opening lecture, described the systems and metasystems of social structures, from the individual through the family, through society as a whole, to the largest possible structure conceivable, and it was this description of relationship that best anticipated the events which were to ensue in the next fourteen days. Gregory Bateson, on the following Monday, discussed the complex systems of competition and mutual dependency that characterize the natural order and how "when the balance swings toward pure competition...the system breaks down (and) some species then follows its Malthusian curve and

top: Leon Redler and Joseph Berke, two of the conference organizers
bottom: On a panel with Jerome Rothenberg
Photos copyright © 2007 by John Haynes
info@johnhaynesphotography.com

top: Scene from Carolee Schneeman's happening
bottom: Julian Beck's panel. (third from right)
Photos copyright © 2007 by John Haynes
info@johnhaynesphotography.com

becomes either a pest or a weed." He examined the role of consciousness in this balance of nature, a role which was to become a constant source of debate. But it was on Tuesday that the real conflict came to the surface, when Stokely Carmichael explained simply that the revolution had, as far as he was concerned, already begun. "We are out to smash American white supremacy... If the Americans want to play Nazis, we will fight them to the death..." When asked whether he would accept help from the hippies, he replied, "Would you come into the black ghettos, and if the cops fire on us get in front of us and throw flowers at the cops?" He declared that the only way the whites could help the Black Power movement was to destroy, on their own, the exploitation of white society, and then, and only then, could any alliance be discussed—an alliance that would have to take place on the black man's terms. His reply to the questions asked him over and over was "What have you done?" His solution was violence.

Carmichael's speech created a storm that was to be repeated many times during the course of the conference. John Gerassi felt that Carmichael's plans were too vague, that what was needed was a tighter structure, an organization, that revolution without planning was doomed from the start. Paul Goodman, contrary to both Gerassi and Carmichael, felt that the solution lay in an adequate understanding of the roots of the system and its problems. A split developed within the ranks of the activists—some feeling there was no room for the luxury of personal analysis, some agreeing that no revolution could be fulfilled if individual problems were not also faced.

One of the most distressing parts of the congress was an often impenetrable barrier that developed on the part of some of the protagonists, an unwillingness to listen to anything that in any way ran counter to their views, or for that matter enlarged them. Although there was much talk of love, of de-mystification, of dialogue, in reality there was often a feeling of tension and violence, of people who listened to one thing one day and were swayed, and then cheered just as loudly the next day for the opposing point of view.

The two people who had the most impact on me personally were Carolee Schneeman and Julian Beck. Beck spoke eloquently about the place of theater in general and the Living Theater in particular in community and social change. An anarchist and pacifist, Beck spoke informally outside the setting of the large meetings, and it was obvious that the people gathered around him really felt connected both to him and to what he was saying.

Carolee introduced me at this early juncture to what it meant to be a woman artist in a political gathering purporting to talk about revolution and change but where, in reality, artists and women were marginalized. Carolee fought hard for her space and for respect for her work and ironically the totality of the conference was best expressed in her kinetic theater happening, "Round House" the last night before the conference disbanded. Using the total area of the theater, she conveyed through the shapes of greased, foil-covered, sweating human bodies silhouetted against pictures of newsreels and scenes from Vietnam, the struggle for contact. In the background, the music of the Beatles, the sounds of the audience, first deadly quiet, then broken here and there both by honest emotional reaction and the noise of people who could not bear, even for an hour, to sit still and listen. The feeling of tension increased and then it died away. The audience was showered with aluminum bottle caps, with light, with music. The end of the happening was a dance. People exchanged parting remarks, and left.

The Dialectics of Liberation was the first time, to my knowledge, that type of conference on such a scale had been attempted, and its failures were failures of excess rather than any lack. Leaving the theater that night I could only think of some of the things that Julian Beck had said the afternoon before—how he had made his dream of community a reality and how with all the trouble, all the confusion, all the horror, how, when the moments of clarity came, they were in a language and with an understanding he had never, as an individual, imagined possible.

TIME

No color. No sound. No movement. No thought.

The moment I realized what had happened, it was gone. Like waking from a dream, but I was already awake and the transition was instantaneous—if you can use the language of time in relation to something that is out of time.

It was in the spring of 1967. I was absorbed in finishing my master's thesis. I had just finished reading *Answer to Job*, Jung's analysis of the psychological development of God in which he sees, as does Rilke, the world as a representation of God in the process of "becoming." I was focusing on the paradox evoked by this idea: *How is it possible for something to be complete, and in the process of completion at the same time?* when, one afternoon, while reading in Paracelsus what I thought was totally unrelated material, I was literally thrown into the answer to my question. For an instant, I actually *experienced* time differently.

I was certain of only one thing: it was no illusion, no hallucination—my experience was real.

When I thought about it later, the only thing I could say by way of explanation was that there exists a parallel time in which we are heading toward a past yet to happen while the future is behind us, already set—this parallel time running simultaneously with time as we ordinarily perceive it. All time, therefore, quite literally *is* contained in the present moment. But even more, the present, being made up of both future and past moments, has no meaning without both. I began to understand the use of paradox in religion and Zen koans, and even in philosophical dialectics—to draw students into a place where their questions can be answered only through direct experience.

I believe what comes from such an occurrence is *raw* experience, having only the meaning that the person experiencing it gives it. It is neutral. I really don't *know* what my experience meant, I could only speculate on it after the fact from who I am.

When I tried to recount what had happened to me later that same evening to a friend, I started to shake and cry uncontrollably. For years that experience was a constant source of frustration. I tried to replicate it and couldn't. I was afraid to talk about it to anyone, afraid they would misinterpret what had happened—if they believed it at all. After a while it began to fade. Soon I would travel to Cuba and the experiences I would have there, however different, would also turn me around and batter ,e, too, if from other directions.

As love had done to me also, when it finally came, when I was up to its demands.

CUBA AND AFTER, 1968 – 1971:
The Movement & Other Revelations

...You could scream it in the streets
and who would listen

But the scream remains the sound of it
like the sound of your voice and those
others like their memory like water

changing as it flows

"MEXICO SALIÓ A CUBA"

The highway from the airport to Mexico City snaked around and through the center of town like Quetzalcoatl, the mythological winged serpent of ancient Toltec lore. Surrounded by concrete, the road connected seamlessly with arched destination markers, both merging into a sky of gray and brown and yellow. I felt I was being driven through the downtown L.A. of my childhood. Color here like color there, dusty, dry, the street names in Spanish, rain a distant memory. Staring straight ahead, I could almost believe I was home again—not in New York, but driving endless Los Angeles freeways, burnt acrid by sun and lack of moisture, that wind through the poorer Mexican sections of downtown, all the way to Olivera Street, a block-long entertainment constructed for the exclusive use of tourists. And I suddenly, desperately, wanted to be back in my own home, in New York, in my own place and not in this throwback to an earlier home, a place I had fled.

As we approached the center of Mexico City, color began to emerge, one hue at a time, a dab of crimson here, the ubiquitous turquoise there, a slash of chartreuse in the background that grew in size as the neighborhoods became progressively wealthier, until at the very center of the city a gigantic park unfolded, green and fresh—Chapultapec Park, "The Grasshopper." As we continued, the green began once again to recede behind us, until everything became concrete again, the streets, the sidewalks, the houses, and we finally arrived at Margaret's block, and everything snapped back into place.

This wasn't Los Angeles, it was Mexico City, and I was soon to meet a friend who would become, as Allen Katzman and Theodore Enslin had before her, one of those people who would constitute my real family.

If I were asked to name the one person who was most responsible for changing the course of my life at that particular time it would be Margaret Randall. Until then Margaret and I had known each other only through correspondence and an occasional conversation on the phone. We had first met when Carol Bergé suggested I send some poems to *El Corno Emplumado,* a literary magazine Margaret co-edited with her then husband, Sergio Mondragon. Margaret immediately accepted three of my poems.

When we started publishing *IKON,* I wrote to Margaret asking if she could write something for the first issue about what was happening in art in Mexico City. She and Sergio sent a column, "Poetry, People and Beans: Mexico City, 1966," which described the isolation of artists in a city of six millions in which "illiteracy—actual and acquired—changes the curve." They wrote that in Mexico City there was "little or no solidarity among the artists themselves," something that was contrary to the political stance of *El Corno.* They noted that almost everyone on their way to Cuba stopped with them and along with the visitors came news that was covered up by more establishment sources. "...people say *things* in different ways; it is often good, sometimes it is not so good but most often this comes from lack of conviction, small growth, unconcluded energies. Something may be missing, but we have come to feel it is not a matter of 'school.'"

This was an idea that surprised me. In those days usually one talked about the separateness of art and the everyday world, the sacrosanct nature of art. I had always thought of poetry and the poet being *apart from*, not *part of*.

Along with these new sentiments were names also new to me: Pablo Neruda and Caesar Vallejo, Ernesto Cardenal, Octavio Paz, Juan Rulfo, Carlos Fuentes—writers from Latin America who were rarely translated in the United States of the early Sixties. These and younger contemporaries, as well as poets from all over the world, filled the bilingual pages of *El Corno*.

By 1967, in the short time between the first issue and third issue of *IKON*, even though both the magazine and I had already begun to change, my knowledge of art and literature extended to almost every place but the continent directly connected to mine.

Margaret and *El Corno* opened the rest of the world to me.

In the third issue of *IKON*, Margaret wrote an article, "A Poet Looks at Cuba Eight Years after the Triumph of the Revolution" in which she discussed her trip in January-February of 1967 to a gathering in Cuba celebrating the centennial of Rubén Darío, another poet whose name I was hearing for the first time. It might have been that article that brought *IKON* to the attention of the Cubans. As a consequence, I was invited to the Cultural Congress of Havana that took place in January of 1968.

At the beginning of December 1967, I received a cryptic call from the Cuban Mission saying that they had approved my request to go to Cuba to attend the Cultural Congress of Havana—a conference I had never heard of, much less sought an invitation to attend—and could I come to the Cuban Mission to discuss my trip. Upon accepting their invitation, I applied for State Department approval to go to Cuba as a journalist, and when approval wasn't forthcoming when it was time for me to leave for the conference, I boarded Air France for Mexico City en route to Cuba. Approval arrived at my apartment three days after the conference began, timed to make it impossible for me to go.

In 1967, an American could go to Cuba through Mexico, but could not return to the United States via Mexico. The only way you could get back to the United States was by way of Czechoslovakia or Spain or, if you really had time and patience, by taking a cargo ship to Canada and re-entering the United States through Canada—a ten- to fourteen-day excursion. I opted to go through Mexico City and return through Spain. That is how I wound up staying with Margaret, who had also been invited to the conference.

If I were to use one word to describe Margaret Randall, it would have to be *vivacity*. She seemed to be constantly in motion. Not frenetic—hers was not a surface energy, but was deeply focused, manifesting itself as strength rather than speed. Her presence was so forceful that it took me a while to realize she was at least three inches shorter than my own five feet, seven inches. She immediately took me in hand as if we had been close friends for years. It was a welcome I didn't expect. She freely shared her home, her friends, her contacts.

While we were waiting for our visas, I spent four days with her and her family playing tourist, visiting the Diego Rivera murals across the street from Alameda Park, eating sandwiches in Chapultapec Park, visiting the Anthropological Museum and the Museum of Fine Arts, and shopping for souvenirs. Sitting by myself one brilliantly sunny afternoon in a sidewalk café, I couldn't help staring at a huge water bottle with a sturdy cork stopper poised on a metal stand that was obviously supposed to indicate the water was sterile and wondering idly if it had been filled using the garden hose that lay lazily dripping water not more than two feet away.

I had taken four highly unsuccessful years of French in high school, followed by a dismal showing during one summer session in college. Although my translations from French to English were always by far the best in the class, I couldn't translate from English to French and I was much too self-conscious to try to speak. When other people spoke, it sounded to me like one long word. Those aptitudes would transfer intact to Spanish.

The evening before we were to leave for Cuba, I awoke

Margaret Randall, with Rodolfo Walsh, writer and journalist, around 1970.
Walsh was murdered on March 25, 1977, by the Argentinean death squads
in Buenos Aires.

from a nap—I had fallen asleep exhausted on Margaret's couch—to see her children Sarah and Gregory and Ximena dancing around me, laughing and pointing. I realized because I couldn't talk to them or answer them in Spanish, they thought I didn't know how to talk at all! I quickly joined in the merriment, laughing and gesturing and dancing happily around the couch.

Going through the airport in Mexico City the next day, I began to get an indication of exactly what going to an "unapproved country" might mean. Even though the Cubans—knowing the trouble an American traveling to their country might get in—didn't stamp our passports, the Mexicans did. They stamped our passports with our destination—*México salió a Cuba* in large letters in a box with a thick black border. And if that weren't sufficient, once we went through immigration, we were divided up into groups of three, placed against a wall, and had our pictures taken. I don't know if we were given numbers to hold in front of us—I seem to remember we were, but that might just be a mental filling in of what it felt like to be treated like a criminal, standing there, backed against a wall, staring into a camera.

If the idea was to make me feel I was doing something suspect, they succeeded. If the idea was to frighten me, they succeeded. But I was also beginning to get annoyed. I knew if I wanted to get on the plane, which seemed farther away all the time, I would have to keep my mouth shut and do what I was told, but intimidation was beginning to have an opposite effect. Truthfully, I didn't know that much about the Cuban revolution beyond the little I had read, and the invitation to travel to Cuba had come as such a surprise I really had no time to acquire much information. My trip was motivated more by curiosity than anything else. Besides, it angered me that as an American citizen my right to travel where I wanted and see how things were for myself was being restricted, particularly when citizens of most of the other countries in the "free" world, including Canada, England and France, could travel to Cuba without restriction.

Cubana Airlines was the farthest airplane out on the tarmac. It seemed like an eternity before we finally arrived at the boarding gate where a Russian turbojet was parked. We sat for what seemed like another interminable length of time waiting for the signal to board the plane. By this time I was really getting nervous, which wasn't helped by a comment by one of the flight attendants to the passenger next to me that they were waiting for the temperature to rise so the plane could take off more easily. I couldn't be sure, but I didn't think they were joking.

Finally, we got the signal and slowly walked the hundred yards or so to the plane and up the metal boarding steps. When the plane took off, I breathed a sigh of relief. Ironically, it was on the "enemy's" plane that I finally felt safe.

CUBA: THE CULTURAL CONGRESS
OF HAVANA

In a poem, words are used to achieve an understanding that can only be grasped by the combinations of words, by their sound, their music, mirroring the full unity of language, the emotion and thought of the poet, the poet's life. All this is a poem. To speak of any element separately is to speak only part of the poem, to understand a part at the expense of the whole. To speak about Cuba during those years, to use words, is to express only part of the picture. The question is how best to express the feeling of it, to convey the experience. A list of facts can never do it.

The Cultural Congress of Havana comprised hundreds of people from almost every country in the world. Its stated purpose was to discuss the problem of culture in the Third World—particularly the steady outward flow of intellectuals from Third World countries and the cultural domination of indigenous culture by the so-called "developed" countries. I say "stated purpose" because many other areas were also opened up for discussion and action. The conference was divided into five commissions: one focusing on political issues, one a discussion of the formation of "the new man," one a discussion of the responsibility of the intellectual to underdeveloped nations, one on mass media, and one on science and technology. To avoid trying to divide my time between all five commissions with the end result of not understanding any of them, I decided to follow one commission through from beginning to end. Since I had a number of friends in the third commission—the responsibility of the intellectual—I decided to attend the second, the one that interested me the most, the formation of the new human.

In the second commission there were about a hundred people. Among the delegates were Hans Magnus

Enszensberger, the poet from West Germany; David Cooper, the psychiatrist from London who was one of the organizers of the Dialectics of Liberation Congress; Robert Matta, a Chilean painter; Alain Jouffroy, a French poet; and, sitting near me, a physical education instructor from Cuba, a teacher from Guinea, and a track star from Czechoslovakia.

The idea of the new human is based on Marx's original conception of the development of a new type of human being in a society in which community is a living fact rather than an ideal, a society without arbitrary divisions between worker, soldier, intellectual. This idea was elaborated on by Che Guevara in *Man and Socialism in Cuba*, originally a letter written to Carlos Quijano, the editor of the Uruguayan newspaper, *Marcha*. In it, Che refutes the negative image of the necessary demise of individuality in a socialist state. The letter contains his now famous quote: "Let me say, with the risk of appearing ridiculous, that the true revolutionary is guided by strong feelings of love. It is impossible to think of an authentic revolutionary without this quality." He adds it is "not a question of how many kilograms of meat are eaten or how many pretty imported things can be bought with present wages. It is rather that the individual feels greater fulfillment, that he has greater inner wealth and many more responsibilities."

This is the exact opposite of Plato's utopia in *The Republic*, which is based on a rigid separation of worker, soldier, and intellectual, with the intellectual, the Guardian, as absolute ruler and decision maker.

I spoke in the commission about art and read a paper on education and was asked immediately how I would apply my ideas to children, to youth, to older people, and if I had a practicable system worked out for experimentation. It was not enough to know what you wanted to do, the real question is: "How do you do it?"

Matta got up and spoke about rain, and being young, and paint, and the rooftops in Chile. "...it is not a question of just backing the revolution; it is the question of being revolutionary. And being revolutionary implies, of course, being free or consequently struggling to achieve freedom..."

Papers were delivered on education, on the rights of women, on the problems of youth, on the "hippies," the "provos," lines from Wilhelm Reich. I learned what Cuba had been like before the revolution, about Batista and how organized crime had dominated the island during the endless hours of discussion, arguments, debates. So many new ideas it was impossible to process them. Too much was happening. Too many faces, languages, too much information. I knew I would have to wait until I got home to sort it all out. Now I could only try to take it in, record what I was hearing and seeing, feeling, sharing.

At the conference I shared a room with Margaret Randall. I hardly remember her being in it—or sleeping. Sometimes I woke up exhausted in the middle of the night to see her just arriving. She had been at yet another discussion, meeting with yet another group of people. Because she had been to Cuba before and spoke fluent Spanish, I met people and saw things I would never have seen by myself or in the company of an official delegation. One day we walked through the streets of the Old City of Havana, just the two of us, with Miguel Barnet, a Cuban writer. Everywhere people greeted us and invited us into their homes to talk and have coffee—a valuable gift since Cubans love coffee and it was rationed and very scarce.

I sensed the same warmth and hospitality I had felt at Margaret's home the afternoon I arrived in Mexico City. At random, we accepted an invitation—an elderly woman who lived in a small room in back of one of the ornate but deteriorating Spanish buildings that line the streets in Old Havana. Upon our acting the "journalists" and asking her what her reaction and the reaction of her friends was to the death of "El Che," she began to cry.

"Third World" Exhibit, Cultural Congress of Havana, 1968

Cultural Congress Delegates, 2nd from left, Aimé Césaire

What was an "objective" question for us was a living memory for her.

Yoruba—or Santaría, the Afro-Cuban version of the original Nigerian oral tradition—is widely known and practiced in Cuba. Miguel took us to a botánica where rows of Eleguas filled a large table. Elegua is the Yoruba Orisha of the crossroads, guardian of the doors, opener of the paths, the mediator who must be invoked before any ritual can begin. Miguel showed us the Yoruba symbols embedded in the Havana sidewalks. I was particularly interested because a good friend in New York, a Puerto Rican drummer, José Quiñones, was a devotee of the religion.

Intrigued by a notice in the newspaper, I attended a puppet theater performance of *The Wizard of Oz*. This was my first contact with the Teatro Guiñol. Their rendition impressed me so much that a year later, when I returned to Havana, I made it a point to go to the Teatro Guiñol again. This time they were performing a new play, *Shango de Ima*, one of the series of plays they were working on to bring to the community an understanding and appreciation of Afro-Cuban culture. Shango is the Orisha of fire, thunder and lightning, of the intellect and of life. *Shango de Ima* is the story of Shango's adolescence, the Yoruba version of how death came into the world. As they had in *The Wizard of Oz*, the troupe combined actors with puppets, using black light, Day-Glo paint, a whole range of imaginative techniques. The people and puppets blended together in such a way that the distinction between the two was blurred. The imagination demonstrated in the productions of the Teatro Guiñol was a sample of the inventiveness of the artists in Cuba in general, particularly in the fields of literature, theater, graphic arts, and film.

Pepe Carril, the author of the play, asked me to translate *Shango* and carry it back to the United States. (Even though it was difficult for me to speak and understand spoken Spanish, I could read and translate very well.) I did as he asked, and *Shango* was published by Doubleday and first performed in 1970 at La Mama ETC and then later at the Nuyorican Poets Café.

Pepe emigrated to the United States in the 70s when homosexuals were again under suspicion in Cuba and died of AIDs in the 1990s in Florida.

The premier performance presented during the conference was the debut of a new ballet, "Carmen," danced by Alicia Alonso. I had never thought of ballet as being particularly sensual—graceful, even athletic, but not sexy. That evening I changed my mind.

Any "free" time we had was spent seeing as much of the Cuban countryside as possible. Driving down one country road, a military truck passed us in the opposite direction, one of the soldiers playing a Conga drum. Circling a new apartment complex in a bus that seemed to be going at least a hundred miles an hour because there was an extra half-hour and this was something you should see. Conversations for hours with people in all parts of the city, the countryside. Sometimes through Margaret, sometimes through another friend who spoke Spanish, sometimes through an official interpreter, sometimes in English, sometimes in a language composed of words and phrases in mixed English, Spanish and French.

Sitting one afternoon in the lobby of the hotel, I began talking to a poet from North Vietnam. Upon hearing I was a poet from New York, he jumped up, "Wait here, I have something to show you." He came back with a book of poems, his favorite, Walt Whitman, in French, bent, dog-eared, and a poem he had written for a Cuban newspaper, about Whitman, and about Vietnam.

Another afternoon, three Americans from SDS and I met with a small delegation of Vietnamese. When they began to praise us for standing up against the war, saying how brave we were, we all began to protest that compared to what they were going through anything we were doing was not worth speaking about. "No," one of them said. "No, you don't understand. We *have* to fight. We have no choice. You don't, yet you support us. Even against your own government. That's why it is so important, so courageous. You support us *by choice.*"

I didn't agree that we were doing anything particularly praiseworthy, but from that day I pledged even more steadfastly to engage in the struggle against the war. It would have been so easy for the Vietnamese to play on our sense of guilt. Instead they appealed to our pride, our compassion. They welcomed us. And, given the circumstances, it was almost too much to bear.

After that there was no way we would let them down.

If a Vietnamese could sit down with me, and talk with me, and greet me, an American, as a friend, how could I ever turn away from anyone, condemn anyone, based solely on a group identity. I also understood for the first time how important it was to organize from a people's pride and not from anger or guilt.

When I arrived back in the United States, I was surprised by the questions people asked. It seemed that what most of them were interested in were details of daily life—not the intellectual discussions of the conference, not politics, but what people looked like, how they dressed, what they ate.

The truth is I hadn't paid much attention to what Cubans were wearing. For the most part, they looked and dressed like people I knew in the United States. The women wore pants more during the day than they did here at the time—partly because they were a staple of the volunteer militia and partly—which I was soon to discover to my dismay—for protection against the elements.

During my travels around the island, I had spent a night at a new resort the Cubans had constructed of wooden palapas on a beautiful lake—you could only go from hut to hut by canoe. But it wasn't a lake, it was a swamp, and the next morning my legs had swollen twice their size. Certain I had blood poisoning, friends rushed me to the nearest hospital where the doctor gave me a shot of antihistamine, laughed, and prescribed...trousers. It seemed I was suffering from multiple mosquito bites so close together you couldn't tell they were bites. From then on, outside Havana, I wore pants most of the time too.

In retrospect, I think the interest here in dress was not superfluous but the result of many harboring the same kinds of stereotypes about Cuba that I had before I went there. They somehow imagined the long lines of dour Cubans sporting Mao jackets.

Nothing could have been less true.

Years sometimes clarify things, sometimes distort them. I am not proposing to analyze or critique the Cuban situation in the years 1968-69. I am trying to convey what it was about the Cuban revolution that inspired a generation of young Americans who were struggling for social change.

In 1968 and 1969 when I was in Cuba, the earlier tragic repressive measures against homosexuals had been mitigated. It is true that even though the camps were closed, gays in Cuba were closeted, but so was I in the United States—this was before Stonewall and the emergence of the Gay Liberation Movement. With the formation of the Gay Liberation Front in 1969, I found myself once again confronting an untenable position. While vigorously joining the struggle here in the United States, I was reluctant to join in a public outcry against Cuba—a revolutionary country under constant siege. Official attitudes in Cuba have since changed, sparked in 1985 by the report that homosexuality should not be treated as a pathology, and almost certainly by the influences of the Gay Liberation struggle in this and other countries. Although it would be naive to think that legislation can automatically change either official or unofficial prejudice.

During my second visit to Cuba the following November, which lasted several months, I had more time to examine both the positive and negative aspects of the revolution. After the Cultural Congress ended, as we were leaving the Havana airport on our return trip, a Norwegian poet I was sitting with said to me, "...before you go to Cuba, it's covered by a blanket of gray. After you land, you leave the grayness behind. There is a clarity about your vision in which the problems as well as the virtues become real."

A clarity that extends beyond Cuba to encompass one's own life as well.

RE-ENTRY

February 1 (1968)

Dear Meg,

Do I really need to say how good it was to get your letter & how much I needed it—no, & that is the best of it. Every day I have been meaning to write so that you would have a letter when you got back, & each day it got harder until your letter opened up again the feelings which had been sustaining me—of the people. I have so far had no obvious problems, there was no trouble at immigration at all—just the desolateness & the city. I got a (short-wave) radio & have been listening every day to it—unable to turn on the TV or listen to the stations around here.

I have already been hard at work—which also has sustained me. It is cold here, gray and constantly raining. I am in excellent spirits & except for that first week, partly from exhaustion—the plane trip was devastating—I arrived home late Monday night—not having been able to sleep on the plane, trying to recover from a severe case of nausea caused by the people on the Iberia flight from Madrid and reading Time magazine and the New York Times.

Meg, again as when I was 19 and had so much to say & didn't know how to write, words deny me. But between the lines are my feelings and my emotion.

> Love, as always,
> Susan

Since American citizens could not re-enter Mexico from Cuba, I chose, along with folksinger Barbara Dane and her husband Irwin Silber, the editor of *Sing Out,* to fly back to the United States via Spain. A four-hour trip from Havana to New York would take two days.

We left Cuba in an old, but very comfortable, World-War-II vintage Britannia prop plane—luxury travel in its time. (The Russian turbojet we had flown from Mexico City to Havana was not equipped to make a transatlantic flight.)

I settled down in a soft wide seat by a small curtained

window, trying to prepare myself for the approximately eight hours it would take to get to our stop-off point for refueling in the Azores. There was much about Cuba that made me feel like I was back in the Fifties, particularly the large, unwieldy cars with their homemade spare parts. Now I felt more like I was on a 1940s movie set. I half expected to see Paul Muni come through the cockpit door dressed in an extravagant pilot's uniform, eager to ask me in some exaggerated movieland manner how I was faring on my long journey home, and perhaps to light two cigarettes, offering one to me.

The Azores only reinforced that fantastic scenario. Dinner found us in a large old-fashioned dining hall with lamp bulbs shaped like candle flames and food served "family style" in large ornate serving plates. The table setting was topped off with decanters of red wine, small round white rolls in covered silver-plated dishes, and cloth napkins properly accordion-folded at each place.

When we finally touched down in Spain, our "flight of fancy" was over.

Since we had more than six hours after our arrival before our connecting flight to New York, Barbara, Irwin and I— the only *Cubana* passengers continuing on to the United States—decided to take a bus into the city. This was during the Franco regime, and we were lucky to be able to leave the airport at all. The following year, along with the photographer Karl Bissinger, I would return to the Madrid airport. Our passports would be confiscated as soon we got off the plane from Cuba, and we would spend the next six hours confined to the passenger waiting room awaiting our flight home—an enclosed space with two curio stalls, one snack bar, and a few rows of hard wooden benches.

The highway to Madrid was lined with American factories, one sign after another in English. It was re-entry into the corporate world. I tried to note the names of the companies as we drove past, but they began to fuse into a continuous blur, until the many buildings seemed like one long building, none distinguishable from the rest.

My mind began to wander, to play back the previous weeks like a projector running in reverse. I saw myself backing up the boarding ramp into the *Cubana Airlines* plane we had just left, walking backwards up the aisle, flying backwards across the ocean, disembarking rear first at the José Martí Airport. Back to the hotel, to the room Margaret and I had shared, to the conference room where I had spent so much time talking, listening, questioning.

Maurice Merleau-Ponty, the French phenomenologist, writes about how we focus in on, and consequently only see, what fits our needs—like a camera lens focusing on a close-up, everything else fading into the background. Before Cuba I would have hardly noticed the factories, the corporate signs, or, when seeing them, they would have merged with the movement of the bus, ignored because they had "nothing to do with me."

For some reason, probably due to tourist propaganda painting vivid pictures of sunny Spain, I thought, even though it was winter, it would be hot in Madrid. All I was wearing was a sundress and sandals, adequate enough dress in daytime Havana in January—if not for Cubans, certainly for someone used to New York winters. When we left the shelter of the airport to board the bus I realized it was closer to 4 then 104. I was freezing. When we got to Madrid, I finally found a store where the shopkeeper cheerfully sold me a pair of white cotton socks for eight dollars. He couldn't hide his delight at taking advantage of a stupid American tourist, and I can't say after what I'd seen on the highway to the city I much blamed him.

It took us another seven hours once we made our Iberia connection to get back to New York. The plane was full of tourists. In the seat directly in front of me, a man and his wife were arguing loudly about the value of their purchases in Spain, about the value of *anything* made outside the United States. I tried to read a copy of *Time* and was startled after a month of reading papers and magazines free of advertising to be staring at a magazine full of ads and page after page of articles about finance and money. *Buy this. Own that. Save for this. Spend on that.* Even the *New York Times* was impossible. By the time we finally got to Kennedy airport, I was so relieved to get off the plane and through customs, I didn't notice what was going on around me.

Then it began to hit me. Where I was, where I had been.

HOME AGAIN

SCA - XXXXXXXXX   January 14, 1968
ARA/CGA - XXXXXXXXXX
Cultural Congress Activities: Susan Sherman

It appears that Susan Sherman was a U.S. Delegate to the Cultural Congress. Miss Sherman reportedly took part in the proceedings of the second commission as a U.S. Delegate. Among her contributions to the high level of the commission's discussion was her explanation of the U.S. "Hippie Movement".
...She travelled via Mexico on December 29th using Passport No. H-747327 (number as reported posing as a "professor".)

SAC, New York   1/19/68

...In view of the subject's travel to Cuba to attend the Cultural Congress held in Havana from January 4 to January 11, 1968, investigation being initiated.

It was early evening before I finally arrived home. Unpacking my suitcase, I lifted out a souvenir cigar box a Cuban friend had given me, made of rich Cuban woods. The smell permeated my room. Here in my room in New York, a smell so identifiable in Havana brought back the presence of that city to me. A smell so thick it took on the texture of memory. A texture which, overlaid on the textures of my present location like a slightly askew double-exposure, helped me to clarify where I now found myself.

It was as if I were seeing New York for the first time, as if someone had stripped film off my eyes, and there the city was before me, stark, without embellishment—the poverty, the racism, the violence. The difference between observing and seeing, between seeing and "seeing."

The world *outside*. Before this trip everything had centered around me, around the pronoun *I*. *I* am afraid of this neighborhood. It is too dirty for *me*. *I* will never live here. *I, me, my, mine.* Like the archaic Ptolemaic system, I had been the world around which everything revolved. The sun, the stars, circling around *me*, never touching me, held by gravity, crystalline, the celestial spheres, the music of the self, *my*self, until now, shocked into recognition of the other, into acknowledging those who had to live on these urban streets, who had no choice, who heretofore were only part of the problem, part of the background. And now, I began to see it, this world *outside,* become part of *it*, rather than seeing it as part of me.

(undated, around February 14,1968)

Dear Meg,

…I miss you a lot. The depression is settling in now after two weeks. Luckily I saw Hans Magnus (Enzenberger) which was quite cheering. ...The magazine keeps me going & the work there is to do. Some poems Ive been writing. & some memories… Theres a clean hate and a clean, good love and theres a hate and a love that burns you & destroys your guts, its the latter that evil thing thats so hard to avoid. That has to be fought day by day... thats the really hard fight and the fight here because its so insidious.

We <u>have</u> to keep in contact. Because of the work & because, if you read my first letter, of the breath it gives me in this cramped city…

I hope youre better now. Please write.

Love,
Susan

To: Director, FBI (105-176672)
From: SAC, NEW YORK (105-9388) (P)
Subject: Susan Ann Sherman
      IS - CUBA
      (00: NY)

...The NYO is presently obtaining additional background information from Hunter College, NYC, to verify SHERMAN's educational credits. NYO confidential informants are also being canvassed in an effort to determine if SHERMAN has been present at any Casa de las Americas (CDLA) functions.
...This case has been afforded continuous investigation in the NYO and results of this investigation will be submitted to the Bureau in a form suitable for dissemination as soon as the above-mentioned investigation is completed.

TO : DIRECTOR, FBI (105-176672)
FROM : SAC, NEW YORK (105-93388)
SUBJECT: SUSAN ANN SHERMAN
      IS - CUBA
      (00:NY)

...Agency checks conducted by the NYO were as follows:

Agency	Contacted	Investigator
xxxxxxxxx	2/26/68	SA xxxxxxxxxxx
xxxxxxxxx	2/27/68	IC xxxxxxxxxxx
Hunter College	2/28/68	SA xxxxxxxxxxx
Board of Education	3/1/68	SA xxxxxxxxxxx
Union Theological Seminary	3/7/68	SA xxxxxxxxxxx

The subject's passport file was reviewed on 2/6/68, by SA xxxxxxxxxxxxxxxxxxxxxxxxxxxxxxxx
Confidential informants mentioned in the LHM contacted during the period 3/1-21/68, are as follows:

Informant	Date Contacted	Contacting Agent
xxxxxxxx	3/1/68	xxxxxxxxxxxxx
xxxxxxxx	3/4/68	xxxxxxxxxxxxx
xxxxxxxx	3/8/68	xxxxxxxxxxxxx
xxxxxxxx	3/14/68	xxxxxxxxxxxxx
xxxxxxxx	3/15/68	xxxxxxxxxxxxx
xxxxxxxx	3/15/68	xxxxxxxxxxxxx
xxxxxxxx	3/1/68	xxxxxxxxxxx
xxxxxxxx	3/19/68	xxxxxxxxxxxxx
xxxxxxxx	3/21/68	xxxxxxxxxxxxx

xxxxxxxx   3/1,21/68 xxxxxxxxxxxxx
xxxxxxxxxxxxxxxxxxxxxxxxxxxxxxxxxxxxxxxxxxxxxxxxxxxxx
xxxxxxxxxxxxxxxxxxxxxxxxxxxxxxxxxxxxxxxxxxxxxxxxxxxxx

My new "seeing" was only the first of many shocks. I was called into school soon after I returned to be told that after reviewing the figures for the fall enrollment (at that point I knew I was in trouble since there was no way they would know how many students would be attending college in the fall in February), they could only offer me one course.

"And it would hardly be worth your while to come in to only teach one course, would it?" Smiling. Hand poised to cross out my name.

"Sure," I responded. "I would rather have at least two, but one course will be fine."

"Oh."

At the end of the following August, since I hadn't heard anything about my class, I called the school to find out when my course would begin. "What course?" was the response. "We don't have you scheduled to teach any course."

FEDERAL BUREAU OF INVESTIGATION
New York, New York
April 9, 1968

Susan Ann Sherman
Internal Security Cuba

...The following descriptive data was obtained from
NY T-4 and a consolidation of data reported in this memorandum:
Name   Susan Ann Sherman
also known as
Susan Anne Sherman,
Susan Sherman
Sex   Female
Race   White – Jewish extraction...

NY 105-93386
II.   AFFILIATION WITH COMMUNIST PARTY
OR MOVEMENT
A.   Evidence of Communist Party Sympathy

A copy of the fall, 1967 Catalogue, Free School of New York, 20 East
14th Street, New York City, describes SUSAN SHERMAN, a member
of the fall semester faculty, as a poet and playwright whose articles
have been published in "Poetry Magazine", "The Nation", "El Corno
Emplumado", and the "Village Voice". SHERMAN's plays have also
been produced "off-off Broadway"...
A suitable photograph of the subject is available in the NYO.

Early one morning, it couldn't have been later than seven-
thirty or eight o'clock, I staggered downstairs half awake to
throw out the garbage. Just as I was lifting the lid, two men
jumped out of a parked car, started snapping my photo and,
before I could react, drove away. We began getting our mail
only once or twice a week, usually on Friday, with a rubber
band around the bundle of letters.

Shortly after that, unhappy with my trip to Cuba and our
plans for future issues, the *IKON* art staff bolted, leaving
Nancy and me to finish the magazine ourselves. As the editor
of *IKON*, my job was to get the material together, edit it, see
it through typesetting, page it, and present it to the group of
artists who would do the graphic design and layout. Then I
could relax. Since that group no longer existed, I now had to
take on some of their work. Since Nancy had a full-time job,
it was too much for her to handle alone.

Following her instructions, I learned to design and lay
out some of the articles, and after three nightmarish weeks,
IKON 5 was finally ready to be shipped to the printer.

I was exhausted.

The next morning soon after the magazine went to press,
I literally couldn't get out of bed. It felt exactly as if I had
torn a muscle on my right side under the ribs. I couldn't
imagine how I could have somehow mysteriously pulled a

NY 105-93388

ADMINISTRATIVE (CONT'D):

Date	Contacted By	Place
2/27/68		
2/4/69		
2/13/69		
2/16/69		

b7 (d)

b7 (d)

SA   was conducted by

b7 (d)

There is no Bureau approved characterization for Movement for a Democratic Society.

The SA who observed subject's magazine office was

b7 (c)

b (l)

It is also recommended that the caption on this case be changed to "SM-MISC", due to subject's lack of activity in SDS. If further information is received in this case which concerns the subject's activity in Cuba, then the caption should be further changed back to "IS-CUBA".

A suitable photograph of the subject is available in the NYO.

b (l)

-B-
(COVER PAGE)

Sample of typical "marked-out" FBI files. Courtesy of the Freedom of Information act.

muscle as I slept. As the day went on I began to feel worse—
the kind of distress you feel when you are coming down with
a bad virus.

April 3, 1968

Dear Meg,

Here is a copy of *IKON* 5 I am rushing you. Will send a dozen by
regular mail.

Can't write too much now, but will write this weekend. Have been
very very sick last few days. Have been at the doctor every day. Am
not sure whats the matter but a great deal of pain in my stomach—
nothing else, just pain. Will let you know when I find out whats
wrong.

...Cant sit up too long so will have to close. Already much progress
on next issue. Have many questions—will write a detailed letter this
weekend.

My love, always,
Susan

The doctor ruled out any muscular problem and decided
because I am a woman it was probably my gall bladder. He
ordered x-rays, which showed a slightly inflamed gall
bladder, and proceeded to give me a prescription for Codeine.

After some initial relief, each pill seemed to make me
feel worse, and by nightfall I felt like my insides were on
fire. There is no other way to describe it. I stopped taking the
medication. It was obvious by then the Codeine was
compounding the problem. But it was too late. I tried to eat.
It was impossible. Nothing offered any relief.

I had never experienced pain with such unrelenting
intensity. There was no respite. All the stories, all the clichés
about hell—they were all true. Hell was here, inside me. I
couldn't move. I couldn't sleep. I could only lie motionless,
a pulse of white hot fire eating me alive.

Nancy, really alarmed now, called the doctor's emergency

number. When he finally returned her call, he said he wouldn't come to our neighborhood at night; the Lower East Side was too dangerous; she should call the emergency room of the nearest hospital.

I don't remember, if I ever knew, what hospital she called, but some intern diagnosed me over the phone as having stomach flu and said it was pointless to bring me in before morning.

I was in too much pain to be moved anyway.

By the time Nancy got off the phone with the emergency room doctor, I was so furious the intensity of my emotion somehow carried me into morning.

By the next afternoon, the pain had subsided enough for me to go to my doctor. He reluctantly conceded that even though I was only in my twenties and I was a woman,, there was a distinct possibility I might have a duodenal ulcer. It finally showed up on x-rays,, and he advised me the normal course of action would be to put me in a hospital, that is, if I had health insurance—which I didn't—but my condition wasn't presently life threatening, and if I had money—which I didn't—he would have me come in every couple of weeks so he could check me out and offer me some reassurance, but since that wasn't the case…

Handing me a prescription for Pro-Banthine and Pheno-barbital, my doctor sent me out into the street, sick and scared—people learned to live with ulcers—instructing me if it were to start bleeding to go to an emergency room. And, also, almost as an aside, if I were to experience really severe symptoms again to come in for another x-ray, a perforated ulcer could kill you.

That afternoon I learned what it was to *consciously* experience an anger so intense, so profound, it seemed to take on a personality of its own. Anger that became a friend, a trusted companion, something I could lean on, turn to, that could be relied upon to motivate me, give me strength. Not a destructive anger, the kind that binds to the hated object. To the contrary, an anger that energizes you for change.

My family had failed me. Many of my friends had failed me. The medical system had failed me. Totally out of proportion to what the Cultural Congress was, what my participation entailed, my government had tracked my steps, leaving a trail of devastation behind.

Now it seemed even my body had turned against me.

I had never thought of myself as a political person. I was an artist, curious above all to experience whatever life set before me. But now it was either fight or succumb to the numbing pain that plagued me constantly.

If I was to be treated as subversive, then subversive I would be.

COMMUNITY

Rows of rented chairs lined Fourth Street, which had been roped off for our first block party. I ran the last of the wires from our bookstore to the projector, closed my eyes for a moment, crossed my fingers and gave the signal to begin. Suddenly the screen lit up and a hundred or so people, mostly block residents, sitting on chairs, curbs, stoops, fire hydrants, cheered and stamped their feet. The flickering figure of Charlie Chaplin took center stage much to the children's delight, followed by a Cuban film documenting the Protest Song Gathering held in August, 1967, with songs from Chile, Australia, Uruguay, Italy, Cuba, Mexico, England, Argentina, the Congo, Vietnam, the United States. Songs in Spanish, French, English, Italian, Portuguese, German rang through the loudspeakers and many from audience joined in— singing, clapping, dancing to music from all over the globe.

April 4, 1968

Dear Meg,

We don't really have a bookstore—we have a store we're sharing and using for storage—now we will take it over and open it as a kind of office/store & sell magazines (*IKON*) ads etc. and also a few other select publications… It's in a nice location, next to Cafe LaMama, so many people pass. Also we will do some other things I will tell you more about when they become feasible (for example, mimeoing and distributing free some good poems &/or articles between magazines). One thing we probably will do is have some poetry readings/folk music etc. once a month or so.

I'm glad you got some money. Did I write you about Charlotte Mormon breaking a violin over Saul Gottlieb's head?

I got Hopscotch by Cortázar and will read it as soon as I finish the book I'm now reading. I've been studiously studying my Spanish every day. I can say Donde hay el telefono with quite a good accent!

My best, and love, always,
Susan

On May 12, 1968, we had celebrated the opening of IKONstore with Jerome Rothenberg reading from his new book *Poland/1931* and Cyrelle Forman performing Jewish soul music from Warsaw, Krakow, Moscow, Kiev, Odessa. From the minute Nancy and I walked into the space at 78 E. 4th Street, we knew it was perfect. It had not been designed to be a storefront, the only window was a vertical oblong two feet wide and about half as tall as the one-story building that housed our new office/bookstore. A distinct disadvantage for a commercial bookstore, but we never succeeded in being very commercial anyway. I don't know how many books we actually sold, although the walls were lined with material very few other bookstores stocked—small press poetry books, magazines and pamphlets. I do remember giving away a lot of books and magazines or selling them at cost. Fortunately we were next door to La Mama and thanks to Ellen Stewart managed to pay most of the rent ($125 month) by designing and printing their programs every week.

The front door opened into two small adjacent rooms, one of which led in its turn into a large square area, perfect for readings and meetings. We even had a tiny bathroom, a necessary amenity our old office had lacked. Our original aim of opening a bookstore so we could "do what we liked" and earn a living didn't exactly work out, but something much better developed from our venture that we had never anticipated—the bookstore put us in touch with the people who lived on the block. Through it, we became part of the community.

Fourth Street between Second and Third Avenues in the Sixties comprised mostly city housing with a large Puerto Rican population. Many afternoons the store provided a safe place for neighborhood children to play. And because their children liked and trusted us, our neighbors came to like and trust us too. We eventually held block meetings and started one of the city's first block associations. One night at a block meeting a man and woman we had never seen before started red-baiting us, pointing at the posters on the walls, holding up a selection of anti-war pamphlets, shouting that our store was obviously run by "commies." Several of our neighbors immediately came to our defense, telling them in no uncertain terms to shut up until they were doing as much for the block as we were, suggesting it might be better if they left altogether. They did, and that was the last we saw of them.

There was always some activity in IKONstore. Groups used it for meetings, and each weekend we sponsored a different event—one evening a string quartet, the next weekend a poetry reading, the next a political discussion.

We had varying luck with equipment. I became quite an expert on the electronic stencil-maker and Gestetner Mimeo we had picked up at a secondhand store on West 20th Street. With the stencil maker we could mimeograph drawings and photographs, and I got to the point that I could print in three colors—one at a time, of course. But nothing went completely smoothly. There was one volunteer in the store who was well-meaning, but it seemed that everything he touched broke. One day he walked in while I was mimeographing some flyers. I had a terrible feeling as I saw him walking toward me asking if I needed help. He was at least five feet from the mimeo, when I heard a gear giving, and then CLINK—something dislodged in the guts of the machine.

Using only the stencil-maker, mimeo, and a pair of scissors, I laid out and printed an anthology of protest writing

Only Humans with Songs to Sing done in collaboration with Dan Georgakas and Smyrna Press. It contained the work of over forty writers including Diane DiPrima, Saul Gottlieb, Will Inman, Dick Lourie, Walter Lowenfels, Marge Piercy, Margaret Randell, John Oliver Simon, musician Phil Corner, and photographer Arthur Tress. Many of the photos were in two colors. We also put out *IKONpaper*, a small magazine, and *Street Sheets*, single sheets of poetry, political articles, cartoons and recipes we gave away on the street.

Nancy became focused on silk-screening. The screens had to be cut by hand, a long and cumbersome process, so for her birthday I bought her a ten-foot-long copy camera so she could make photo silk-screens as well as photostats, half-tones, and negatives. It was quite a camera, made of wood and polished brass with a huge bellows. It had to have been made at the turn of the century. The copy stand took six 200-watt bulbs, so the first thing that happened when we finally got the camera into the apartment was to set the fuse box smoking, resulting in an expenditure of several hundred dollars to have the wiring changed. Our next fiasco consisted of buying special emulsion film to make photo silk-screens and , because it seemed logical to remove the exposed portion with hot water, we washed the first batch down the bathtub drain, losing over four hours' work and managing to add a plumber's bill to our already mounting expenses.

Along with our daytime jobs, we worked continuously either at the bookstore or at home on the magazine. I was seldom without pain. Medicine held it in check, but it was always there, a dull ache, sometimes flaring up, sometimes subsiding. It was beginning to wear me down. We were putting the sixth issue of *IKON* together. It was to be devoted to the Cuban Cultural Congress.

April 5, 1968

Dear Meg,

It is pleasant and warm out today. I might go out later for a little walk. Except for rides up to the doctor I really havent been out for the last week. We were afraid there would be a lot of violence in the city yesterday because of Martin Luther King's assassination. The last month has been totally chaotic—with Johnson's "announcement" he would not run & that he would cut down the bombing in Vietnam (I trust you can imagine how much) and then this, and then the rioting in Washington yesterday. The right wing is pushing for tight restrictions "law and order" based now on King's death. The kind of laws, of course, that would have stopped King, not his assassin.

The unfortunate thing in all this is that it is completely without any kind of responsible leadership. Right now, its just a big mess here. Thats one reason I wanted to get out of the city this summer—its already started and when it does it will hit without knowledge or direction. But it is impossible to say what will happen—the mood is ugly on all sides and anything is possible. They have passed very strong New York State anti-inciting-to-violence laws (whatever that means)—I'll write more about things as they come up. Since speculation and analysis are impossible about all you can do is report. I plan to take part in the April 27th demonstration—the Chicago demonstrations are fast turning into fiascos because of Johnson's statements and the irresponsibility of the "Yippee" organizing. The SDS people at this point are telling people to stay away. I'm going to try to get in touch with (Dave) Dellinger next week and talk to him a little about what is going on and what he thinks is the best course of action.

I am supposed to give a lecture on Monday at DayTop (a center for drug addicts) on Cuba. So far I have given a talk at the Free University which turned out quite well and the first of the month will give an evening of Cuban poetry and music for the Folklore Center.

...I miss you a lot Meg. Hugo and Nancy have been wonderfully faithful. Nancy took over most of my shit work last week when I was laid under. Everyone else left.
I hope you are well. My best and love always,
Susan

One of the greatest misconceptions about the movement was that it was humorless. Often humor was the only way to get through. Thanks in good part to the influence of the Hippies, I gave up my beat-period black and movement fatigue green for tie-dye and bright colors. Drugs were taboo—mostly because they were an easy way for the authorities to arrest political people using a nonpolitical reason—although if they really wanted to, they could always plant them. Since I was on medication for my stomach, even drinking was out, although it would be many years before I would stop smoking.

When Timothy Leary arrived in New York to do a week-long series of talks on Buddhism, thinking to take a break, Nancy and I crossed Second Avenue to the Fillmore East, a rock-&-roll haven, where we had been once before to see an early performance of a very young Joan Baez. I had decided to put aside any negative feelings I had about Leary and approach his lecture with an open mind. After all, the stories I had heard about him were all hearsay. Allen Katzman had told me a dreadful story about an encounter he had with him when Leary visited the East Village Other. One night they all went out partying and Leary slipped a drunk on the Bowery LSD and waited for him to freak out. After that Allen wanted nothing to do with him.

There was another rumor circulating that at the beginning of his lectures at the Fillmore someone had jumped on the stage high on acid and Leary had called the police. "Turn on, tune in, drop out"—*turn on, tune in, turn'm in Leary* as far as I was concerned.

Unfortunately, as the evening progressed, it looked as if my worst fears would be realized. The accompanying light show by Jackie Cassen and Rudi Stern was incredible and worth staying for, but Leary babbled incessantly through every moment of it as if he were lecturing to infants.

(Silhouette of Buddha as baby.) Here is Buddha as a baby. (Silhouette of an old man with cane.) See Buddha growing old. (Just in case we missed the point.) See, there is an old man with a cane. (Swirling blood corpuscles.) Something about internal reality.

By now, I was not only annoyed, I was bored, but the light show still held me. From what I understood, Buddhists didn't mean examining physical organs and the blood stream when they talked about a spiritual quest. Leary was once a behavioral psychologist, and as far as I could see he still was.

When the auditorium lights went back up, Leary turned to the audience and said very seriously, "Just pretend for sixty seconds I am the wisest man on earth." "I don't have that good an imagination," I said to Nancy as I headed as fast as I could to the nearest exit.

During those years, political and alternative organizations and people were under constant attack. Sometimes the assaults were verbal; often they were much more serious. We had some protection, though it came from a most unexpected source. While La Mama was on one side of the store, the other side was occupied by The 82 Club, a transvestite nightclub that catered mostly to straight people from outlying parts of the city—mostly Staten Island and Queens—and was rumored to be run by the mob. The doorman was a moonlighting or retired police sergeant, we never figured out which. We chatted with him and occasionally gave him small gifts. Given the circumstances of the times we had relatively few problems, either from the police or from burglars. I suspect most of our good fortune was thanks to him.

August 4, 1968

Dear Meg,

...The weather here continues hot and oppressive. Every week new incidents. Plus many bombings of pro-Cuban places. The last incident The Daily Worker. Which makes 16 in all.

Last week a brick was thrown through the store window. We had the window replaced & now will have to get a gate (about $80) or face the consequences of paying for the next broken window (at least $90). I'm just hoping the landlord doesn't kick us out—he hasn't renewed our lease yet so legally he can throw us out if he wishes to.

My best, and love, as always,
Susan

August 31, 1968

Dear Meg,

I really cant thank you enough for your beautiful letter so I wont even begin to try—you have no idea how much it meant to me...

...Things continue happening so fast & are getting so bad here. The mess at Chicago was unbelievable. I see now how people get trapped. They just dont believe what is happening. 20 reporters beaten up. A delegate to the convention dragged off the floor—one other beaten and arrested in the hall not to speak of the incredible brutality to the students and protesters which was somewhat expected. & Humprey saying they all deserved it. I saw his speech on TV & the man is not only everything he is accused of being he is also really crazy.

But this is all very hard to write. I will write a long letter again soon.

My best, and love, as always,
Susan

Chaos doesn't result from change; it results when the disintegration of a system is not accompanied by the birth of a new vision. Chaos is not brought about by rebellion; it is brought about by the absence of political struggle.

It was political struggle that most characterized for me the years from 1968 until the middle 70s As Berkeley had signaled one turning point for me, and Cuba another, soon the Stonewall uprising would signal a third, a new direction which would culminate in the 5th Street Women's Building action on New Years Eve, 1970.

THE DOCTOR & FIDEL

Upon my return to New York, I began writing to René Vallejo, Fidel's doctor. I had met him the previous January at the Cultural Congress. Fidel had attended a reception for the delegates the closing night of the Congress and Vallejo was, as usual, by his side. With his short-cropped white beard and snow-white hair, skin deeply tanned and smooth (he was only forty-four), he looked the image of an Indian holy man, however incongruously dressed in a comandante's uniform with a pistol strapped to his side. Compassionate, a doctor, it was rumored that Vallejo was a spiritualist who followed the Yoruba orishas—one of the reasons he had never joined the Communist Party. He had left a comfortable life to go into the mountains and devote himself to making the revolution and making the revolution work. It was said that he and Celia Sanchez were the only two people Fidel totally trusted.

Vallejo spoke perfect English, and we chatted together for a few minutes after I formally met Fidel. I told him a little about myself and *IKON*. Margaret told me later he had come by our hotel room the next day to see me and pick up copies of the magazine, but I had already left for New York. About two weeks after I returned home, I got a phone call from the Cuban mission that they had a letter for me.

That was the beginning of our correspondence.

I would stop by the mission every month or so to pick up a letter from him and after a while it became obvious to the Cubans at the mission how sick I was and that I wasn't getting better. In his next letter Vallejo invited me to return to Cuba to enter the hospital there for treatment. Finally, when I was no longer working and *IKON 6,* the issue devoted to the Cultural Congress, was finished, I felt I could accept his invitation.

Monday

Dearest Meg,

So good to get your letter—was terribly worried about you. Tana de Gamez reported that 200 student leaders were executed by the government and over 2000 arrested and we were frantic.

Have been feeling very badly again—no didn't finish article. Am trying to get it done for the next issue of *IKON*, and will send a copy in a day or so—if it is too late, then I understand and am sorry not to get it in sooner. I have only been up and around a couple of hours a day.

Will be in Mexico on Nov. 6, will write & give details when I get them. Am trying to get the next issue together now. No money came through as yet. Am anxious to get away for a while & try to get myself back together. It has been quite something here—nothing like there though—just tedious, tremendously frustrating, waiting.

It will be so good to see you again. So much better than I can say.

Love, always,
Susan

The two days I spent with Margaret, when I arrived in Mexico City, unlike my previous visit, were extremely tense. The situation there for students and political activists was getting desperate. Tana de Gamez's account referred to the student protest at Tlatelolco, the Plaza of Three Cultures, on the night of October 2nd, 1968. It was reported later that over 1,000 people had been murdered by government special forces shooting into an unarmed demonstration.

In July of 1969, while plans were being formulated for a commemoration of the first anniversary of the inception of the student movement, the repression would hit Margaret and her family. She would be forced to flee Mexico. She would live for many years in exile in Cuba and Nicaragua, finally returning home to Albuquerque, New Mexico, her childhood home, from 1947 to 1955, and with the aid of the Center for

Constitutional Rights win an extended struggle to stay in the United States.

Only a short time before I arrived in Mexico City, Karen Wald and a small group trying to fly to Cuba were kidnapped from the Mexico City airport and driven all night to the Mexico/Texas border. Because of that, Margaret and Robert Cohen, the man she was living with then, waited at the airport restaurant to make sure I was all right. She and Robert weren't sure what was happening and were frightened for me, as I was for them, but with much more reason. I would only be in Mexico City two days. It was their home.

As passengers exiting Mexico went through customs, officials were questioning them about where they had stayed in Mexico City. Since I was on my way to Cuba, I didn't want to get Margaret in trouble by saying I had been staying with her, but I really didn't know the city all that well, so I wasn't sure what I was going to say. The woman in front of me gave them the name of a hotel in the center of town so I just gave the name of the same hotel when the official asked me where I had stayed. He stared at me and repeated his question. I repeated my answer. "You're lying," he screamed, and proceeded to hit me full across the face with my passport. It landed on the ground and I bent down and picked it up without a word, numb by now, both physically and emotionally. "That's where I stayed," I repeated again quietly. He scowled and waved me through. By the time I got to the *Cubana* boarding gate, I was shaking and soaking wet.

As the plane began its slow descent into the Jose Martí Airport, it was impossible to see past the collage of color, the Caribbean a seamless blue, Cuba patterned in various shades of green. There was still no sign of cities or houses, no other color beyond brilliant emerald hues stretching in all directions.

I had no idea what would greet me when I arrived. The Cubans at the embassy in Mexico City, pleasant enough, but noncommittal, gave me a sheet of paper with my visa on it, smiled, and wished me a good trip. My only contact in Cuba was Vallejo, so I expected he would send someone to meet me at the airport, or at least have left some instructions for me when I arrived.

When the plane finally finished taxiing into the airport, they wheeled the boarding ramp into position for us to disembark. I saw a jeep pull up under the wing of the plane. Looking out the window, I saw Vallejo get out of the jeep and position himself at the bottom of the ramp. It is impossible to describe what it meant seeing him standing there. I looked around the plane, curious to see who he had come to meet.

He was waiting for me.

Vallejo checked me into the National Hospital where I would stay for a month, until one day, examining me, he declared me well enough for a surprise he had prepared for me. The next evening, I would meet with "the prime minister." What I didn't expect was the meeting with Fidel would take place in an almost deserted basketball court in the middle of the night...

It was almost midnight when I was interrupted by a knock at the door. An army sergeant, very short and very serious, stood there, beckoning to me.

"Where are we going?"

Silence.

I repeated my question.

He shook his head impatiently and repeatedly waved his hand for me to hurry. I tagged along behind him until we reached an old army jeep that would have looked out of place in any other cosmopolitan city, but was a common sight in the Havana of 1969.

In Havana, even well after midnight, people spilled onto sidewalks blazing with noise and music. The activity on the street and the brightness of the city's lights gave the illusion

René Vallejo Ortiz

of daylight, but as we headed away from the city we truly entered night. Driving deeper into the stillness that surrounded the city, I could easily imagine never stopping, driving forever on the silent country roads.

The stadium was a silhouette cut out of charcoal, the kind of emptiness you can only feel in the countryside, never under ubiquitous city lights. As we drove toward the huge edifice, at first I had no idea what it was we were approaching. As we drove closer, I could see soldiers with submachine guns standing behind the pillars fronting the building. It was an eerie but not a frightening sight. When the sergeant led me inside, I realized I was in a gymnasium. And, with the exception of four or five other people who were seated directly opposite the entrance, it was completely deserted. When I turned around to try once again to communicate with my guide, I realized he was gone.

Now I really was puzzled. I circled the rows of empty seats until I reached a vacant seat next to a well-dressed woman, probably in her middle or late forties. Sitting down next to her, I ventured a smile. Her response was to glare down at me through large orange-rimmed glasses, in one well-timed gesture making me feel very young, very poorly dressed and very out of place. Even though at this point my Spanish had almost completely deserted me, I was able to ask where the bathroom was.

Relieved to have a specific goal, I fairly raced toward my destination and once there spent some time staring into the large mirror that lined one entire wall, wondering what I was doing in this stadium, in this city, in Cuba. Home so far away, not only quantitatively, in miles, but qualitatively—that other world being the antithesis of everything this one represented to me.

This trip to Cuba would be much longer than the first, almost four months, and already I had begun to see the complications of the ongoing process which is the Cuban revolution. But even more than what was happening in Cuba on this warm Caribbean night in December of 1968 was what it meant to me, to all of us who were struggling so hard to understand who we were, what we were about, what we were about to do, not here, but hundreds of miles away, where snow was falling, thick and mean.

What Cuba meant to me that night, very simply, was possibility—that change could occur, regardless of the odds.

I pulled myself together and returned to my seat. It was now close to two o'clock in the morning—and still nothing seemed to be happening. Then, just when I was contemplating returning to my bathroom sanctuary, a side door opened and several men in makeshift basketball shorts and tank top uniforms trickled into the stadium. The woman seated next to me smugly pointed out her husband—the minister of something important. I didn't quite catch what she was saying. It turned out she could speak English after all.

She explained that at least once a month all the government ministers met in the middle of the night—the only free time most of them had—and played basketball. And often Fidel joined in.

Fidel. Was that what I was doing here? But there was no Fidel, just a dozen young and middle-aged out-of-shape men.

It was now well after two o'clock and I had sat through a rather interesting hour of basketball—considering the players, not the game—when the minister's wife, as I now referred to her, pointed to the door and whispered conspiratorially, "Fidel."

I saw Vallejo first. It was hard to miss him. A large man, he seemed to even tower over Fidel. Fidel stopped to greet each of the ministers, who were now crowding around him as he made his way across the basketball court, Vallejo pointing him in my direction.

The game resumed as the two men climbed the stairs below our seats, and the next thing I knew they were standing directly in front of me. At a reception the previous year, my introduction to Fidel had been quite brief, no more than a smile and a handshake. That meeting had taken no more than two minutes. I expected this one would be the same.

I was wrong. This meeting would last almost an hour, and unlike the first, when I was too panicked to take in much of anything, this time I had several minutes to observe the two men as they walked toward me.

What struck me first were Fidel's eyes. They radiated isolation, a loneliness that was as overwhelming as it was unexpected. It was a spontaneous observation on my part, and the last thing I would have thought of *a priori* if called on to describe a man like Fidel Castro. Although it should not have seemed surprising, considering the number of people close to him who had been killed, not the least of whom was Che Guevara only two years before.

As soon as we began to speak, I realized what was so compelling about the man. His charisma wasn't based on physical presence or power or even the passion of his infamous speeches. Each time I spoke, he waited for a few moments, head tilted to one side, as if mulling over what I had said before he replied. I could see why people were so drawn to him—a person who listens.

If it was an illusion, it was an irresistible one.

Out of politeness, I tried speaking in Spanish and realized after two or three sentences that out of politeness, I should stop. Vallejo translated what I said to Fidel and then his responses to me. I had heard that Fidel understands English perfectly but prefers not to show that he does in public.

He began by asking how I was feeling, how I found my stay in the hospital, whether they had treated me well, what I thought about Cuban doctors. Laughing as he spoke, because, of course, it was Vallejo, his doctor, who had been mine.

I replied that I was feeling better and was grateful for the way they had cared for me and that my stay in the hospital had been an education in Cuban culture as much as in Cuban medicine. I recounted how, in an attempt to get me to stay on in Cuba, some of the older women patients—there were many country women on my floor being treated for ulcerated legs—had literally dragged me first into the room of a fifteen-year-old boy with tuberculosis and then into the room of an eighty-year-old man, the only available eligible bachelors, to try to get me married to a Cuban.

I also wasn't used to the informality of the hospital. Many patients had turned closets into impromptu kitchens complete with hot plates and coffee, and those who were ambulatory helped to serve meals to the patients who were bedridden. The nurses thought nothing of sitting on the patients' beds, smoking and chatting. The last week I was there, the doctors and nurses even put on a magic show for the patients, who were generous with both their compliments and insults.

All of which immeasurably helped the healing process.

Fidel laughed and asked how I thought things were going in the United States. He was very curious about the student movement, the status of demonstrations against the Vietnam War, how artists and poets were reacting to those events, and just about my life in New York in general.

I hastened to assure him I was no expert, but would do my best to answer his questions. In actuality, our conversation turned not so much on the conflict between people involved in anti-war protest and the American authorities, but on how we, the participants in that amorphous entity called *the movement*, were getting on with each other.

I tried to describe some of the nuances of *the movement*, how hard it was to overcome the years of bias exacerbated by those in whose interest it was that we not join together. How we were struggling within a very large, complex situation, the "we" itself being so many different peoples with different and sometimes conflicting strategies and agendas. I felt it an important notion for me to get across, since so much of the information the Cubans had about America was insulated and simplistic, coming mostly from sectarian groups.

Fidel reminded me that he landed originally with no more

than a dozen comrades and made a revolution, that in comparison our movement in the United States was huge. Of course, Cuba has a population of about fourteen million as compared to then over 250 million in the United States, but Vallejo had said to me they expected reform here not revolution—they had had great hopes if Kennedy had lived that some accommodation could have been reached.

Vallejo now shook his head and interjected how tragic it was that government and business could solve so many problems, stop so much dissent and bloodshed by only giving an inch or two, and they wouldn't even do that.

Then, as suddenly as they had arrived they left, exiting through a rear door. I felt a little tug at my elbow and turned to see the minister's wife looking unabashedly shocked. In an extremely friendly and ingenuous voice, she remarked politely that she had no idea I was a friend of the prime minister and gave me her card saying if I ever needed anything to just give her a call. She was cut short by the sergeant appearing at my side to take me home.

. By the time we got back to Havana, the sky was already beginning to lighten and now it was the countryside that was coming alive with color and sound, while Havana was gray and deserted, the very picture of a city asleep.

It is difficult to separate present feelings from past experience. To avoid the pressure to in hindsight be critical, objective, sophisticated—which usually translates into pretending you don't care. It is even harder to avoid pitfalls of nostalgia and remember how difficult and complex a time we were living in then.

Vallejo became for me the symbol of everything I admired in a human being. I never, in all the time I was in Cuba, met anyone who didn't like and respect him, including people who were opposed to the revolution and Fidel. I loved Vallejo, and the fact that I knew how much he cared for me and respected me gave me great courage and brought me through many difficult days. I wish I still had his letters to guide me now, but they were stolen from my files in New York in that most complicated of times. I'm sure, like anyone else, he had his shortcomings, but I never got a chance to see them.

Before I left Cuba that winter, Vallejo invited me to return the following year for another extended visit. I was back in New York waiting to finalize the details of my return trip when I heard he had died as the result of a stroke while playing basketball, perhaps on the very court where he had brought Fidel to meet me. Even now I wonder what my life might be like if Vallejo hadn't died. It would be over two decades before I would return to a very different Cuba from an equally different United States.

CUBA: THE COUNTRYSIDE, THE PEOPLE

A kaleidoscope of images and impressions: huge pre-fabricated walls stacked against each other like giant cards; trees lining the highway, the branches overhead thick with leaves even the bright Cuban sun couldn't penetrate; long stretches of acrid dust, hot, stifling; a mountain range stripped bare of foliage, millions of trees cut down by the Spanish, until even the climate changed, and where there was once rain, it rains no longer, and now the replanting, tree by tree, to bring back the moisture, to bring back fertility to the land. Each scene following the other so rapidly, it is hard to remember in what sequence they occurred.

After spending a month in the hospital, I was eager to get out of Havana. I was feeling much better, and I wanted to see more of Cuba, particularly the western part of the island, where the revolution began. Maria, who worked with the Cuban agency in charge of helping foreign visitors, made arrangements to accompany me to Santiago de Cuba, Las Villas, Cienfuegos, Santa Clara, and the Isle of Youth.

Leaving Havana, we were greeted by a huge billboard with REVOLUTION in white and blue letters—the E the Cuban flag, blue stripes with a single star on a background of red. Our first stop was a Cuban landmark, a beach with black sand made of pulverized marble, studded with palm trees, straight and tall in the sun. A few miles down the road, we visited a small fishing village; a fisherman mending his lobster trap looked up, smiled, gestured at my camera for me to take his picture.

It was all very interesting and relaxing, but I felt I still hadn't seen what was different in Cuba "ten years after the revolution."

That soon changed. Our next stop was a fruit orchard on the Isle of Youth where young people were doing volunteer work.

The island was being used for experimental communities to see if it really was possible to eliminate money and live up to the motto, *From each according to their ability, to each according to their need.*

Two young men, bearded, with guns at their sides, showed me around. Except in places like this where people were doing volunteer work, beards and long hair were frowned upon—just as autonomous black and women's organizations were discouraged. I understood the motivation to bring everyone together under one identity, to eliminate the divisions that had been so deep among the Cuban people before the revolution, but I also knew from the struggles going on in my own country that many believed a new sense of identity must be forged by those who have been denied their identity before such a reconciliation is possible—the psychopathology of centuries of racism and sexism.

It felt like it was over one hundred degrees even though it was December. One of the young men proudly handed me a glass of fresh-squeezed orange juice from their own trees, and thirsty as I was, I almost spat it out. The glass was almost a third full of sugar. The Cubans put sugar in everything. One doctor even went so far as to suggest a teaspoon of sugar once an hour as a cure for diarrhea. After finishing my "juice" gracefully, I was taken on a tour around the farm. The women had written *las guerrillas* with pebbles in front of their main tent. On a whim, I challenged one of the women to a game of ping-pong—I was school champion in the fifth grade and felt I could at least hold my own. She accepted happily and the rest of her friends crowded around excitedly as we played and laughed together for more than two hours. Now we were no longer strangers. Now we could really communicate.

The month I had spent in the hospital only Vallejo spoke English and the old women on the floor made it one of their tasks to tutor me in Spanish, which they did with an unrelenting patience. Consequently both my comprehension and my ability to communicate, although far from perfect, had improved a hundredfold. Particularly when I wasn't in a situation that made me nervous or self-conscious.

Next, Maria and I visited a cement factory in Cienfuegos. It was only half-built—like much of the other construction we had seen in Cuba. Because of the US blockade and embargo, the Cubans were having trouble getting cement. A factory like this would produce much needed building materials. Once *it* was built.

The stop after that was a real stop. A dozen long-horned cows were grazing in the middle of the road and refused to be rushed, either by the honking of our horn or the two cowboys riding beside them. So we waited, and waited. And waited. Then onward to an electrical power plant—again, under construction.

It seemed like the whole country was under construction.

Like the cement factory, the electrical plant was by the water. Surrounded by countryside, there was not another building for miles, just brush and trees. The plant was one story, of poured cement, painted cream and tan in long, flat lines. It looked more like an apartment complex than a factory.

The electric plant might have looked like an apartment complex, but the difference became evident when we visited a new housing project. Each complex of four buildings had its own school and day care center and encircled a garden and playground. (The children were inside taking a nap— their tennis shoes, more than two dozen pairs, decorated a stone block.) Using a modular method of construction, a building could be put together in less than two weeks. The prefabricated walls were delivered to the site with all the wiring and pipes already built into them. After being assembled, each apartment front was painted a different bright color to give it variety. This was accompanied by a "re-education program" to teach new tenants how to live in their new homes. Each apartment had a new stove and refrigerator, but some of the occupants, who had never had

Tenth Anniversary Celebration: January 1, 1969

Orange cooperative on Isle of Youth   *Photo: Karl Bissinger*

Women in tobacco factory in Havana   *Photo: Margaret Randall*
bottom: Backyard in Havana   *Photo: Susan Sherman*

an electric stove before, were discovered putting charcoal in the burners and grilling their food. Creative, but also quite messy and very dangerous.

On the road we passed the shacks that the new complexes were replacing. Wooden shanties with no electricity or running water. Little more than sheds. I couldn't help but think of the overcrowded tenements at home and the housing projects that looked more like prisons than people's homes.

San Andrés is located almost in the center of Las Villas province. A four-hour drive from Havana, it is perhaps one of the most beautiful valleys in Cuba. But most important, San Andrés was one of the many experimental "integral" communities in Cuba begun in the Sixties. In the schools, students were housed, fed, and clothed. From an early age they took part in the running and care of their schools, helping to make their schools completely self-sufficient. Each student spent the morning growing the food the school consumed as well as helping in the construction of new facilities whenever possible.

The school administrators were young—the director of the high school we visited was twenty-four. The teachers' ages averaged between eighteen and twenty-two. During my visit, I spent two hours in a fifth-grade class discussing world events with students who often caught me off guard with the astuteness of their remarks and the difficulty of their questions.

Noticing broken chairs and desks in the next school we visited, a junior high, I asked why some of the school equipment was damaged, since the school was only two years old. The director explained that most of the older children had never been to school before this school was built, and many of them needed time to adjust to their new situation. When I then asked about discipline, the director was surprised and said that if they punished a child, the child would grow to hate the school and think of it as a prison.

When students did something destructive, it was explained to them why what they did was wrong and if that didn't work it was explained over again, not only by the teacher or administrator, but by other students. The director concluded, "Things have improved considerably in the last two years. We are very proud of our school."

By coincidence the next day we visited a site where Fidel was dedicating a new school, behind him the slogan, *To Study Is The Most Extraordinary, Essential And Profound Necessity.* It began to rain, but no one moved. Those who had umbrellas shared them, others just stood there as the rain began to come down harder. By the time Fidel finished his speech, rain was dripping from his hair and beard. On the way back to the city, our bus got stuck in the mud, and everyone climbed down and pushed until we freed it. I arrived back in Havana, tired, muddy, wet, but in good spirits, and feeling better than I had in months.

During our travels, Maria and I became good friends. Maria's father was Italian; her mother, Cuban. They had a small home in Havana, and one night, soon after we returned, they invited me to dinner for a special treat, her father's favorite dish— spaghetti with tomato sauce made with huge chunks of pork. A unique blending of cultures. Maria invited me to join her and her husband for Christmas. They planned to use their vacation to visit his family in Bayamo, a small town with a long revolutionary history in the province of Oriente. I accepted gratefully. This, at last, would be my chance to spend some time with a family in the Cuban countryside.

A week before Christmas, or more precisely before the annual Christmas feast—presents are exchanged ten days later during Three Kings Day—we flew to Santiago de Cuba where we would get our connection to Bayamo. We took the few hours between planes to wander around Santiago. The first thing that attracted my attention was a small crowd gathered around what turned out to be a children's circus set up in a parking lot. The ring was covered with straw, surrounded by bleachers. The only act seemed to be three cowboys, a clown, and a couple of trained dogs. The dogs jumped through a number of small hoops, tails wagging, while the clown, dressed in a torn tuxedo, circled the ring, dancing and playing a small violin much to the delight of the children. All this took place against the backdrop of a tall building decorated with large letters that spelled out VENCEREMOS (We Shall Win).

Then, finally, Bayamo. Maria's parents lived about two miles from the center of town in the old part of the city, their home one of a row of small one-story poured-concrete houses with red tiled roofs and tall arched doorways and windows. A young boy greeted us, galloping up and down the street, playing horse with a sugar cane stalk and rope. Children were running in and out the front door. Both Maria's in-laws were retired, and the house seemed to be perpetually full of children. Everybody in the neighborhood seemed to know each other, and their children were free to wander and play where they would.

In Cuba it is hard to separate out attitudes that are a direct result of the revolution from attitudes that are the result of being in any small town, from attitudes that are typically Cuban. All of them taken together differentiated the Cuban revolution from that of any other socialist country.

One thing immediately noticeable about the Cubans was their lack of cynicism. They might be critical—some overly so—but they weren't sarcastic. I will never forget one afternoon in the hotel elevator in Havana when Jules Feiffer, the cartoonist, was shocked and not a little dismayed when he reduced his young interpreter to tears with some "humorous" remarks he was making about Cuba.

My first "close encounter" in Bayamo was with an annoyed hen who took umbrage when I went to the bathroom, which was a concrete enclosed outhouse attached to the main building, and obviously one of her favorite nesting places.

As I was sitting there quietly thinking about whatever one thinks about in a privy, I was startled by at least six pounds of feathers and beak plopping abruptly into my lap. A small scuffle ensued from which both the hen and I managed to emerge frazzled but unharmed. My second encounter came a day later when I was chased out of the yard by an incensed adolescent chicken with hardly any feathers at all who, flapping her wings violently, headed straight for my ankles. I must admit I felt no guilt about eating chicken for dinner that night, or for secretly hoping it was one of my feathered enemies. I doubted it was though—one was too young, and the other too tough.

The next morning, the family insisted on waking me up at five in the morning to see the pride of the community—the new dam. Even though I was exhausted, it would have been extremely impolite to refuse, so mustering as much enthusiasm as I could, I climbed into the old jeep that would be our main means of transportation.

We arrived, after much bumping and scraping over dirt roads, at what looked like a small reservoir, with the water flowing over an incline that couldn't have been more than a few feet high. Looking around for the dam, I was told that *was* the dam, and tried to look suitably impressed. Like many island nations, one of Cuba's main problems is maintaining an adequate power supply—the reason it became so dependent on the Soviet Union for oil. That problem was partially solved in Bayamo by the most popular means of travel, one that took advantage of the original source of horse power—the horse and buggy. This was a ride I looked forward to with a great deal of anticipation only to find myself suffering from a credible case of motion sickness!

Each family had been given a pig the first of the preceding year to fatten up for their Christmas feast. A handy recycling vehicle. The pig ate the garbage. The family ate the pig. The day before the big feast was to take place I was taken for a walk along the river which I found out later was a ruse to keep me from hearing the pig being butchered. The last time I had seen the poor animal, it could hardly move. It squatted over its dinner, rolls of fat hanging from its bones. The next time I saw it, its skin had been fried into crisp appetizers and it was being prepared for an all day barbeque. The men took turns rotating its giant body over a pit that had been dug especially for the occasion.

The main meal was eaten around noon, after which everyone retired under mosquito nets for an hour's nap. I learned to cook plátanos—green bananas, sliced, fried, and then, when half done, smashed flat with a stone and fried again. Every couple of days the mother would roast a new batch of Cuban coffee. As the beans were toasting in an iron pan over an open flame, handfuls of sugar were thrown into the beans and caramelized—hence the incredible (and delicious) sweetness of the strong dark mixture.

There was a lot less shortage of foodstuffs in the country than in the city since people raised their own chickens and helped themselves to coffee beans in the fields. Also many other goods like shoes and clothes were more readily available. At the time there was an attempt to try to get Cubans to move from Havana into the outlying regions, so more goods were being distributed in those areas. In a country of a few millions, almost a third of the population was squeezed into Havana.

Shortly after arriving back in Havana, I was picked up to go to another of Fidel's speeches. I was almost killed when the brakes went out on our car. I was sitting in the front seat when I suddenly, completely intuitively, looked down at the floor. It was as if time slowed almost to a stop. In slow motion, I saw the driver's foot push into the brake. The car didn't stop. He pumped his foot up and down on the brake. Nothing. We were going about ninety miles an hour. There was traffic stopped in front of us, a truck was coming full speed down the adjacent lane, so there was no way he could

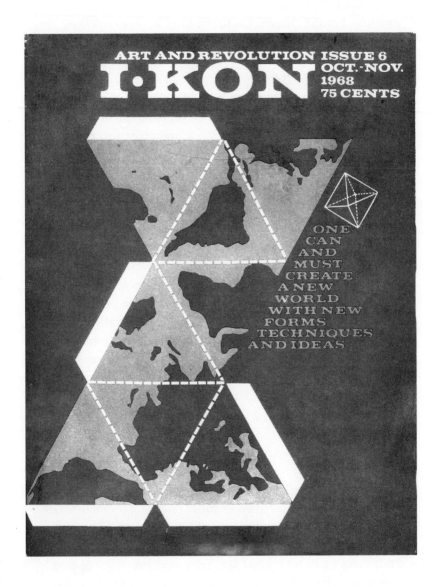

IKON 6: Devoted to the Cultural Congress. Adapted from a cover of
TriContinental Magazine.

bypass the stalled traffic. On our side of the road was a sharp incline, barring that escape route. Then he did something I would never have expected. He put his foot full on the gas and going at breakneck speed headed for a field on our left, crossing in front of the oncoming truck with only inches to spare. Once on the dirt, he took his foot off the gas and maneuvered us across the field until the car finally came to a halt. After an hour we were rescued and continued our trip on horseback.

I spent almost four months in Cuba this second trip, the bulk of it outside Havana, much of it in the country, where the revolution started and was most in evidence. Although I was almost always with other people during my first trip to the Cultural Congress, this time, a little less than a year later, I spent all my time either with Cubans or alone. I seldom saw other Americans or foreigners until the beginning of January when the tenth anniversary of the Revolution was celebrated—or the tenth anniversary of the rebellion as the Cubans preferred to put it, seeing the revolution as an ongoing process. During that time, I could go where I wanted, when I wanted, and speak to anyone I wanted. There were times when I was on my own when I actually wished someone was tagging along with me.

Because I was in Cuba for a longer period of time, I began to confront some of the problems of the revolution as well as being much more appreciative of its virtues. Along with the caring, hospitality, idealism, and support there was also the pettiness, narrow-mindedness, and lack of privacy that probably exists in any small community. I also recognize that there was a lot I didn't see. Years of oppression can also breed paranoia, clannishness, and violence. I knew this well enough from my own family.

This being said, I found in this revolutionary Cuba a compassion and willingness to work toward a common goal of creating a truly revolutionary society at great personal cost. The Cubans had taken me in and healed me. Above all else, these are the impressions I would take home with me.

And now it was time for me to go home. I was well, and Nancy was struggling to get out the seventh issue of *IKON*. We would soon get another rude awakening. But this time I would be better prepared.

THE STRUGGLE ESCALATES

When I returned from Cuba that winter I brought music back with me, and music in turn brought Cuba back to me. It was not the slogans or scenery, scholarly papers, or large convocations, it was the memory of people I carried back with me, reborn in the recordings of the Canción Protesta (the protest song festival), Afro-Cuban chants, the music from *Shango de Ima*, the popular music albums given me by Cuban friends—with artists like Benny Moré and Mercedita Valdes, the Canción Nueva—the new music of struggle and discovery. I searched second-hand record stores for Lena Horne's rendition of "Now," used for the soundtrack of Santiago Alvarez's film of the same name so vividly portraying the civil rights struggle in the United States. "Now," an American song I heard first in Cuba, a song that was banned from some radio stations in the US as too incendiary.

And the other music—the hum of the mimeograph machine late into the night, the noise of crowds hurrying past the store to get to theatrical performances at LaMama ETC merging with the loud crescendo of political debates going on in the main room of IKONbooks. Poets with their own particular songs, neighborhood children slamming in and out the front door, and sometimes the quiet no-sound of solitude and work.

Ho Ho Ho Chi Minh, the NLF Is Going to Win now joined the cries for peace. The ideology of evolutionary change, of reform, began to be replaced by the slogan, *Revolution in Our Time*. This change of attitude was neither facetious nor was it sudden. Nor was it relegated only to the war in Vietnam. Those in struggle knew the war *had* come home. Everywhere movements for "national liberation" were taking place: in the African American community, the Puerto Rican community, Chinatown, the American Indian Movement. On the TV almost every night one could view atrocities against the Vietnamese, GIs being sent home maimed or dead, police brutality on the streets of the United States. The Vietnam Veterans Against the War was a powerful force in the anti-war movement. Emotionally charged films like *Hearts & Minds* (1974) and even earlier more reserved and detailed historical documentaries like Emil D'Antonio's *Vietnam in the Year of the Pig* (1969) documented the details and history of the war. Progressive newsreel collectives and Liberation News Service graphically documented national as well as international struggles. People were traveling to Vietnam and Cuba and bringing back first-hand reports.

The message was out.

The moral dilemma in the face of all this evidence was agonizing. Even reading and studying and thinking to the point of exhaustion didn't lead to any foolproof answers about strategy or tactics. However, no matter how we acted out our response, many of us felt it all boiled down to one very clear question: Did we want to directly or indirectly be complicit in genocide?

Choice is simple only in retrospect, only in the kindness and generosity of memory. From the first demonstration in Berkeley through all that followed, it was impossible to know for certain if what you were doing was the correct action to bring about the changes you thought just and fair. There was always that nagging doubt that your actions might have exactly the opposite effect. But what was not in doubt was the necessity to act.

There is absolutely no way to understand the period of the middle Sixties to the end of the Vietnam War in the Seventies unless one understands that *everything*, including music gatherings like Woodstock, took place against a backdrop of war, both at home and abroad.

Work. Day after day. Night after night. Subsistence work in the daytime doing a series of odd jobs for little pay. And then, after work, more work. Setting up political discussions, poetry readings, musical events, community organizing, hour after endless hour at the mimeo machine cranking out leaflets, flyers. Then, later at home, middle of the night, putting together what would turn out to be the last issue of the first series of *IKON*. Often working all night—one night mimeographing ten thousand flyers for a Black Panther Party event. Ten thousand flyers. I thought it was impossible, if not for me, for the machine, but we, the two of us, kept on going. Ten thousand flyers, twenty reams of paper, neatly stacked in boxes waiting to go to their final destination—the street.

What did I think about? There was no time to think about anything but the work we were doing. What did I feel? There was no time to feel anything except how I would find the energy, the drive, to continue, to keep on doing what I felt so desperately needed to be done.

One afternoon I joined with a small group at the Federal Courthouse at Foley Square to support Dionne Donghi, a member of the Weathermen (later the Weatherpeople) we felt had been unjustly arrested. She had been betrayed by her boyfriend, who turned out to be a police informer. A young woman, in her early twenties, small, maybe five foot one or two, slight, little more than one hundred pounds, shackled, she entered the courtroom guarded by four burly plain clothes agents, who, by comparison, seemed huge. On my way out of the courthouse one of the agents was leaning against the door, smoking. As I passed by, he took the cigarette out of his mouth, muttered, "Scum," and slowly and deliberately spat full in my face.

It was during this time I met Joan Hamilton and Sonia Marerro. I met Joan through Flo Kennedy, an African American civil rights lawyer and feminist, who had hired me to help her because she needed a friend she could trust to "clean up" her office—which meant sorting through and throwing away boxes of papers. Sonia was a young woman, no more than seventeen or eighteen at the time, who was active in the Puerto Rican independence movement. She had worked with Juan Mari Bras in Puerto Rico and was writing for the Puerto Rican Independista Newspaper *Claridad*. Both Joan and Sonia became invaluable co-workers and close and dear friends. Sonia would die prematurely in her late thirties of complications due to breast cancer.

At the end of 1968, under the tutelage of Tom Wodezki and continuing the tradition of the Free School, the Alternate U. opened its doors. I began teaching there, but as we approached the Seventies, the students were more into psychology and encounter groups than politics or philosophy. While the writing course I offered did well, I tried to offer a course in dialectical philosophy from Plato to Mao that failed to get enough interested takers. However, it was at the Alternate U. that I met Zayd Malik Shakur, who was Minister of Culture of the New York Black Panther Party. Zayd was a slight but wiry man, quietly determined. I never remember him, even when angry, raising his voice. Joan, Nancy, and I worked with him as part of the National Committee to Combat Fascism which was formed to publicize the Panther's School Breakfast Program and Community Control of Police, two main programs of the Panther Party in New York. Our work consisted of putting together flyers, posters, and doing whatever publicity was needed. Contrary to popular belief, the Panthers, at least in New York, were mainly concerned with creating school breakfast programs, combating police brutality, and getting corruption and drugs out of their neighborhoods.

In 1973, Zayd Malik Shakur and Assata Shakur were stopped by state troopers on the New Jersey turnpike. A shootout ensued. Assata was badly wounded and Zayd was killed.

One night we did a benefit for the Panthers in the bookstore. The store was filled to capacity. We had bought a couple of cases of beer and some potato chips and other snack foods. Two men who were obviously agents sat in the small front room the entire evening and managed to drink their way through almost half a case of beer and eat most of the food. They had absolutely no interest in either the program that was going on in the other room or who was attending it. I thought them a little stupid and fairly harmless, if obnoxious.

I didn't know how wrong I was.

In 1977, I sent for my files from the FBI, CIA, and State Department through the Freedom of Information Act as part of a class action lawsuit that was being considered by the Women's Rights Project of the ACLU. Of the 29 documents listed by the CIA, 26 were totally excluded; one quarter of my FBI files were denied, while the rest were almost totally blacked out. As far as I could *see* there was nothing relevant to my activities in the women's movement. The files seemed to deal primarily with the years directly following my first trip to Cuba in December of 1967. At one point there was a recommendation by the New York Office that I not be interviewed and my file be closed because "it is believed her position as a magazine editor and writer might lead to embarrassment of the Bureau."

But my file wasn't closed. The most damaging visible entry was the totally untrue allegation that I had been clandestinely "traveling back and forth from Cuba...under express instructions of Eldridge Cleaver and others." At the time Cleaver, chairman of the New York Black Panther Party, was living in exile somewhere in Cuba and the New York Panther 21 were on trial for conspiracy to blow up (of all the ridiculous charges) the Bronx Botanical Gardens. (They were later acquitted by a jury in forty-five minutes after spending two years in jail awaiting trial.) COINTELPRO—the FBI's covert campaign of infiltration and disinformation against

For mercy has a human heart, pity a human face. . . .
william blake

FASCISM HAS NEITHER

NATIONAL COMMITTEE TO COMBAT FASCISM

Mimeographed poster: National Committee to Combat Fascism

the movement, particularly the black movement—was at its zenith.

I could only marvel at what other fictions might be hidden in the dozens of censored pages. And the damage they had done.

When *IKON 7* came back from the printers, we sent it to our distributors. At that point we were printing 10,000 copies of the magazine and paying for it solely with money from sales and from our salaries—mostly Nancy's. Within a space of one week, all three of our distributors sent us letters saying they no longer wished to distribute *IKON* and sent us back #7 along with #6—the issue on the Cuban Cultural Conference—which, until then unbeknownst to us, had not even been unpacked. The 500 copies of Issue 6 we had sent to Margaret in Mexico never arrived.

That was the end of the first series of *IKON*. There was no way economically that we could continue. In 1982, I restarted the magazine as a feminist publication with a $5000 insurance policy left me by my stepfather when he died. The "second series" of *IKON* magazine ceased publication in 1994.

Psychological warfare. Insidious attacks that attempted to, and in many cases did, break the most important thread on which any movement, or relationship, is based—trust. Trust, a simple five letter word. A word much maligned and much overused. And yet so much hinged on it. Who could you trust? What could you trust? Could you even trust yourself?

Perhaps the hardest thing to deal with was that many people, including some of my close friends, just didn't believe what was happening to us. To the point where, at times, I began to lose faith in my own experience. Whether it related to my encounter with a different perception of time, the loss of my job, the loss of the magazine, my travels to Cuba, my intuition about people, my writing, or FBI surveillance.

Warfare. In Vietnam and at home.

The one good thing about seeing my file was that it confirmed what I had suspected about government surveillance—some of which was obvious, at least to us. It had to be, otherwise it wouldn't have been intimidating, and intimidation was most often the main motive. Besides the agents who devoured all our edibles at the Panther benefit, one weekend, going to Sonia's apartment building to pick up her mail while she was on vacation, I bumped into two FBI agents standing in front of the mailboxes. They looked like they had just come out of central casting. One wore a beige raincoat; the other, a gray suit. They were over six feet tall, with short cropped hair. In a tenement building on East Fifth Street between Avenues A & B in the late Sixties, they couldn't have stood out more. I pretended I was looking for someone's name on the bell and hurriedly left, trying to look as casual as possible.

But most cases weren't nearly as clear. It was one thing to intimidate, another to provoke, to infiltrate, to set people against each other, to destroy. It wasn't necessary for an agent to order someone to terminate your job, to drop distribution of a magazine. All they had to do was to show up and say they were investigating you.

I trusted Joan, and I trusted Sonia. But there was one terrible moment when the trust between Nancy and me was broken.

Sometimes it was necessary for me to follow my instincts about a person or a group, even at the risk of being wrong, but always erring on the side of caution, especially when it came to other people's lives. A short while after Nancy and I broke up, I was staying temporarily at a friend's. A woman named Virginia was causing a lot of dissention, mainly in women's political groups, and many people were convinced she was an agent—or at the very least she was acting like one. Nancy, ever ready to take up the cause of the underdog, befriended her.

I didn't like Virginia. She had the same kind of aura that had earlier caused me instinctively to forbid an outlandish character named Prince Crazy access to the bookstore, even though he was very popular. It turned out later he was a paid informer and was responsible for several people being arrested. In Virgina's case, for Nancy's sake, I stayed out of the controversy.

One night Nancy and Virginia kept at me until three in the morning insisting that I vouch for her. I couldn't do it. I had continued my political work and if there was the slightest chance that what was being said about Virginia was true, I couldn't put any of my friends at risk. Nancy took it personally. Our relationship was never the same.

It might well be that history is written in terms of its "leaders," but it was the tens, if not hundreds, if not hundreds of thousands of people who were active, in whatever capacity they struggled, who really constituted *The Movement*, not the dozen or so names thrown up into prominence—sometimes deservedly, sometimes not. People mobilized for many different reasons, some with good and some with selfish intentions. But I felt then, and feel even more strongly now, that by far the vast majority of those engaged in struggle were *and are* motivated by a genuine desire to act against injustice and to move our society into a more humane and equitable direction.

This was the movement I joined in the Sixties, the movement I fought for, struggled together with. A struggle that manifested itself in every aspect of my life, in every waking hour and sometimes even when asleep.

THE 5TH STREET WOMEN'S BUILDING

"Our Hands, Our Feet, Our Minds, Our Bodies are Tools for Change"
—The 5th Street Women's Building Motto

Snow was falling steadily. It was almost midnight, but the reflection of moonlight on the slick white streets made it seem more like early morning, that crossroads between dawn and waking when the distinction is blurred between what is imagined and what is real. I was standing in front of an old station wagon parked on a deserted street corner.

It was New Year's Eve, 1970.

June Arnold, in her capacity as head of the Women's Center Literature Committee, and I, as one of those unofficially representing housing advocacy, had almost unloaded the last of the supplies one hundred women would need to complete our takeover of the now-abandoned city-owned building located at 330 East Fifth Street between First and Second Avenues. It had formerly been a school and welfare building/women's shelter

The storm was a mixed blessing. The building was almost directly across from the Ninth Precinct Police Station, and we were simultaneously hidden by the thickly falling snow and waist-high snow drifts and vividly outlined against their stark white background. No one knew how the police would react if they saw us. June and I stood guard as the women climbed, one at a time, through the broken panes of glass. We handed supplies to each woman in turn until we were sure all the women were safely inside. Then carefully, almost ritualistically, we locked the doors of June's car and, following our sisters' lead, crawled through the side windows into the bare first floor corridor. We continued up a flight of stairs into the huge second floor area which many would call home for the next two weeks, as the clock carried us triumphantly into 1971, and the gutted walls of the abandoned building echoed our victorious shouts of "Happy New Year" and "Sisters United Will Never Be Defeated."

There were few of us who went through the 5th Street Women's Building that night and the following two weeks who were not profoundly affected by it. Up until that time, I was one of those who had never really thought of gender as having much logical causality in my life. I understood that things "happened to me" because of my political activism, because I was a poet, because I was queer, but not because I was a woman.

The night of the takeover, I was thirty-one years old. My first sexual relationship with a woman had been a decade before. I had been living with a woman for more than four years. My trips to Cuba had cemented my stance outside the mainstream of society, and it was via this route that I now began my approach toward feminism along with other women who were also beginning to realize that fundamental social change had to include a change in the relationship between the sexes, and that included a new perspective on the issue of homosexuality.

The 5th Street Women's Building was my first all-women action. It was because of this action that I became friends with June Arnold, who would go on to co-found Daughters, Inc.—one of the first woman-run alternative presses publishing only women's work—and help establish the Women's Coffee House.

Reeni Goldin, a co-worker at the Cooper Square Tenants Council where I was employed at the time, had the original idea for the action. It was the result of Reeni's commitment to finding a way to combine feminism with the growing squatters' movement. Seeking feminist support, she searched the Women's Center card files for women interested in "housing activism." She found only one name—June's. They put out a call together, and the response was overwhelming.

The 5ᵗʰ Street Women's Building was planned as a feminist/ squatters' action to take over a property that was being neglected and turn it into a women's sanctuary providing among other services a health care center, a Gimme Woman's Shelter, a food co-op, an Inter-Arts Center, a clothing and book exchange, a lesbian center, a temporary halfway house for homeless women, and a feminist school. Other long-range projects proposed included a welfare women's group, housing action group, and a center for alcoholic women.

At the planning meetings, what I remember most clearly was the commitment, careful planning and noncompetitive spirit of the women in general—and two women in particular who were blatantly making out with each other, much to others' and, I must admit, my own annoyance. No doubt fueled in my case by no small amount of self-consciousness. Thanks to the Women's Building and Stonewall that would soon change. Only a year and seven months before the takeover, the last weekend of June, 1969, the police had raided the Stonewall Inn, a gay bar on Christopher Street in the West Village. People had protested and demonstrated for three days, and the gay liberation movement was born.

It was a time of profound questioning for all of us. Many of the women would explore relationships with other women for the first time. Others, although remaining in relationships with men, would form close emotional relationships with women and investigate their own identity in a way they would never have imagined. At the time, women's liberation was a growing movement, strong on many fronts. Women in SDS had raised the issue of their decidedly shabby treatment as early as 1965. But for many women in New York, the building served as a focal point for exploring these new affirmations.

The women who came together around the 5ᵗʰ Street Building were mostly individuals and small groups of friends who each brought their own agenda with them and found, in this enormous open space bounded only by the long rows of sleeping bags and scattered belongings, that as long as they could find other people to help them or they could somehow get it together by themselves, they could put their ideas into action in a place free of sectarian ideas and organizations. Most had heard about the building either from the call put out through the Women's Center or IKON bookstore or by word of mouth. Each day different women passed through the building, staying for an hour, a day, and some for the duration of the time we were there. Consequently, there were many activities going on simultaneously in a kind of organized chaos.

One of the first things we did after taking over the building was to change the name on the portable heater June and Reeni had brought. The M in Mister Heater was painted over with an S and it became "Sister Heater," our official mascot. Kitty litter was brought in, dumped in large garbage bags, and impromptu toilets set up.

Where the pre-action meetings had branched off into "consciousness-raising" sessions as well as strategy sessions, once we took over the building the meetings were centered around practical details. Now we had to deal with specific tasks like maintaining the bathrooms, replacing light bulbs, making sure the kerosene heater was handled safely—fire being the main excuse the city was using in threatening to evict us. City officials by this time had realized what was happening in the building and were trying to figure out the best way to get rid of us.

Many of the women's projects were realized during the short period of time the building was actually occupied. There were karate classes, a book exchange, a food co-op, and a clothing exchange. There was a children's theater workshop. But what was most essential was the day-to-day living, working, acting together in direct community action, where circumstances forced us not only to learn to make compromises but, most important, because of our obvious vulnerability, to protect each other.

Our self-image, our identity, determines both the choices we make and whether we act on them, whether we think we are capable of acting on our own or for each other's behalf. That is why many political struggles have first been struggles bound up with identity politics and have strong nationalistic elements. Many of us saw the growing lesbian/feminist movement in the early Seventies as a continuation of the struggle we had been engaged in during the Sixties—one which spoke to what kind of society we would like to see replace an oppressive structure bolstered by the triad of racism, sexism and economic exploitation.

We believed that one of the most outrageous actions women could take was to throw in their lot with each other and refuse "heterosexual privilege"—to be shielded and protected by men. "Lesbian" was a label used to make women afraid to fight for their rights, so it was a term that had to be "demystified" and embraced as a form of defiance. "Dyke" and "queer" were later used when the term "lesbian" was felt to be too mild.

Consequently, large numbers of women were attracted to each other who under other circumstances might not have been. Many others discovered a newfound sense of their own sexuality, and many lesbians who had been closeted came out in this compelling atmosphere of women supporting and loving women as political action. Other women, like myself, found political meaning in a life we had been living for years.

In the 5th Street Women's Building all of these dynamics were present, but in an atmosphere of support and tolerance, even among the many women who were and stayed heterosexual. However, some organizations like NOW— today a very different organization with different attitudes— rather than dealing with the issue of homophobia, refused to support the building because of the presence of the lesbian center, feeling that women coming out openly as lesbians created a diversion and would turn off their constituency, an argument alarmingly similar to the one that had earlier been used in some progressive organizations against the women's movement in general.

The consciousness-raising meetings that were started as an adjunct to our political action meetings prior to the takeover, although interesting to me intellectually in terms of their codifying women's issues and problems, didn't hold me emotionally. The world they described didn't seem to have much to do with me in a personal way, although politically I could appreciate their importance.

In retrospect, I can see how I began unconsciously to understand events in my own life differently as a result of the discussions we had individually and as a group, and I can recognize how much my disassociation from many of the issues discussed was due to my inability to relate to my own condition as a woman.

Conversely, I was put off by some of the rhetoric and theoretical posturing, a familiar experience after years of political activism. At one meeting two young white women we had never seen before, who said they were welfare mothers, totally disrupted plans that had been worked on for days, without anyone questioning who they actually were. In fact, we never saw them again after that one meeting.

Even some of the more positive aspects of the action sometimes worked to our detriment. Because there were so many different women passing back and forth through the building and because we were concerned about abolishing hierarchical authority, when the necessity arose to make a quick decision—which was an ever-present possibility in a situation where the police could break in at any minute—we often found ourselves in a situation difficult to successfully resolve.

Imagine a large open room, peeling institutional paint, huge sheets of plastic covering broken panes of glass, "Sister Heater" directly in the middle of the room, women scattered cross-legged on the floor looking very serious, very anxious, very nervous, and poised in front of them an infuriated Florence Kennedy—the civil rights lawyer and African American activist we had asked to help us with our fight against eviction by the city. Scanning the room, her voice barely audible, very softly, very slowly, very menacingly, deliberately emphasizing each word, she said, as if to each woman individually, "I have memorized the face of every woman in this room and not one of you should ever, and I mean *ever*, ask for my help again."

Hyperbole, to say the least, but it had its intended effect.

What had so angered Flo was her advice on how to most effectively act against the city's threatened retaking of the building had been greeted by a curt statement that she would not be allowed to do or say anything publicly until the appropriate meetings had been held and the women had decided, by consensus, whether or not to follow her instructions. Which could take time. Which we didn't have.

I felt caught squarely in the middle. Flo was a good friend, as well as an experienced lawyer, and had put a lot of time and effort into helping us. On the other hand, I also understood the women's position and one of our major problems—there was no one individual or one consistent group of women who had authority. The attendance at most meetings comprised whoever happened to be in the building at that particular moment, a varied and varying group.

The 5th Street Women's Building action lasted a little short of two weeks before it ended in a blatant and under-reported act of police brutality against women.

Several women had volunteered to participate in a planned arrest using the tactic of nonviolent resistance.

GIMME WOMANS SHELTER
MUJERES ~ WOMEN

HEMOS COGIDO ESTE EDIFICIO PARA NOSOTRAS

NECESITAMOS SU APOYO AHORA
LA CIUDAD NOS QUIERE ECHAR

UNASEN A NOSOTRAS HOY,
MAÑANA Y SIEMPRE.
ABIERTO 24 HORAS
FELIZ AÑO NUEVO 1971

AHORA TENEMOS
UN NURSERY
INTERCAMBIO DE
ROPAS Y LIBROS
COOPERATIVA DE
ALIMENTOS
CLASES DE ARTES
PRONTO TENDREMOS
SERVICIO DE SALUD GRATIS
TRATAMIENTO PARA
ADICTAS
ESTUDIOS PARA MUJERES
CENTRO DE LESBIANAS
OTRAS NECESIDADES
DE LA COMMUNIDAD

330 E.5
1-2 Ave.

WE HAVE TAKEN THIS BUILDING FOR ALL OF US

WE NEED YOUR SUPPORT NOW
THE CITY IS TRYING TO EVICT US

JOIN US TONIGHT,
TOMORROW and FOREVER
OPEN 24 HOURS
HAPPY NEW YEAR 1971

SERVICES FOR SISTERS NOW
CHILD CARE
CLOTHING EXCHANGE
BOOK EXCHANGE
FOOD CO-OP
ARTS WORKSHOPS
SERVICES COMING SOON
FREE HEALTH CARE
DRUG TREATMENT
FEMINIST SCHOOL
LESBIAN CENTER
OTHER COMMUNITY
NEEDS

WOMEN THIS BUILDING IS YOURS

NOTHING IS SECRET ANYMORE

As one hundred women silently crawled through a window on New Years Eve all of a sudden a loud shout of 'POWER TO THE PEOPLE' rang across the street. Startled women turned around, raising their fists, gesturing Shhh and saw a black sister and brother on the front fire escape of a building across the street.

WHAT HAPPENED ON FIFTH STREET?

On New Years Eve over 100 women from almost every womens liberation group in New York City (and many not in any group) took over and held an abandoned city-owned building on East Fifth Street across from the Ninth Precinct between First and Second Avenues. Formerly a womens shelter and welfare building, it was abandoned by the city for lack of funds four years ago.

It is really huge - each of the five floors has one gymnasium sized room and five smaller rooms. The walls are

OFF THE CITY

The city's first suggestion was for the women to leave the building and then they would begin negotiations. Sure. Power to the people who have sense enough to stay in their own building. Seize the time. Seize the space. And don't let go.

CHILDCARE

A temporary drop-in childcare center is functioning now while women are working on a huge room on the first floor. This room has access to a kitchen and a courtyard and will be used for 24 HOUR childcare. Possibly cubicles (about 16) once used for offices on either side of the

Clipping: from article on Gimme Womans Shelter.
Reprinted from RAT. January 1971, Issue #19

Everything had supposedly been thoroughly worked out with representatives of the city and the police force—it was our intention to continue our fight in the courts and through the media. The alternative presented to us was a forcible evacuation of the building which might result in serious injury to many of the women, the loss of all the materials collected, and all the work we had put into the building.

Unfortunately, many of the organizers were not seasoned in police tactics. Having been in a fair number of demonstrations by that time, I was appalled to discover that the planners of the rally that would accompany the arrests had chosen for the rally's location the parking lot behind the building, an isolated area accessible by only one entrance—a small driveway the width of two cars. I protested the choice of location, but was overruled. The rationale was there would be no danger because both the location and time had been cleared by the police.

When the time for the rally came, I had a horrible feeling that my worst fears were about to be confirmed. There was only that one escape route out of an area jammed with at least two hundred women. I started frantically urging women to get out of the area even if it meant stopping the rally. They ignored my warning as the alarmist fantasy of someone who had been in the Left too long and in turn warned me to be quiet or leave. Seeing my attempt to change things was futile, I moved quickly to the rear of the rally, perched half in and half out of the small entrance along with some other women who looked as worried as I did.

In the front of the building, the preplanned arrests proceeded in an orderly manner. I was just about to gratefully concede I *had* been paranoid when I noticed the last of the press had left and quite a few women were still lined up waiting to speak.

Suddenly, two police cars sped toward the parking lot entrance. Now I yelled as loudly as I could, helped along by the other women beside me, all of us in tandem shouting for everyone to get out. But it was too late. Only a dozen of us managed to get through before the exit was effectively blocked by the cars swerving around and parking sideways across the driveway, effectively leaving room for only one woman at a time to get through.

Pandemonium broke out as the police began to beat and drag women across the rough pebbles of the parking lot alley as they battled frantically to get through the small escape space. The street was absolute chaos. I finally got to a phone when a woman living in a basement apartment adjacent to the police station saw what was happening and let me in. I called every lawyer and doctor and media person I knew, hoping their presence would stop the violence. More than anything else I remember the sound—the thud of the police clubs hitting arms and legs and backs, and women screaming, both in terror and in rage.

Later at the police station, one of the women who had been arrested earlier said she heard the police laughing about how they had taken care of those "hippies" and "dykes" and "commies" who had occupied the 5th Street building.

That afternoon gave many women a quick and horrific education in what it meant to go against the established system. They learned that being a woman was no protection when you were considered "the other," no longer "one of us."

Even in a feminist setting, we could not avoid the complexities of the society we had left behind. We carried those problems and contradictions along with us. But with all of its complications, the pioneering spirit of the 5th Street Women's action and its successful attempt to coordinate feminism with concrete community activism made it historically significant.

The real import of the 5th Street Women's Building finally was what we as women brought away with us—what it meant in our everyday lives. The action was, after all, the collective effort of individual women, each with a name and a unique history, with the courage or the foolhardiness to be able to accept conflict and contradiction, even within our own ranks, and to continue to passionately struggle for change.

For the women occupying the premises, it was our own personal version of the Stonewall uprising—our political initiation under fire as feminists, planning and carrying out a radical political action. Women, together, we bonded in that ten-day occupation—eating, sleeping, working as a community in close to zero temperatures, holding the building, and each other.

HOME
New York City, 2006

The magic lies in understanding the secret
of return of falling back   as well as
breaking free

RETURN

How many years does it take to unravel the complexities of a journey that propelled a child of first-generation immigrant parents from a working-class neighborhood in Philadelphia to the mythic avenues of 1940s Hollywood, through the transformative years of Berkeley to the avant-garde art world of New York, to a Cuban movie theater filled with Vietnamese students and the turbulence of the Sixties?

There is no such thing as an unnoticed event, a trivial subject. Our lives are made up mostly of an accumulation of small incidents: the crowded supermarket on a Saturday afternoon, a baby crying at three o'clock in the morning in an upstairs apartment, people marching miles on dirty New York streets protesting an unjust war, the touch of a lover's hand. Seemingly different, each one alone, a detail, but taken together events with major importance, turning history to new directions.

During the summer of 1976, one month before I would turn thirty-seven, I made my way back to California, the place I had once called home. I was booked for a series of readings in Berkeley and Oakland, but first I would visit Los Angeles. After fifteen years of absence, I finally felt strong enough to face the place that had shamed and nurtured and frightened me both into silence and into words.

On the face of it, returning home was a matter of steps—walking across a threshold, into a room. But it had taken me more than a decade to prepare for it. A young woman going through the Mexico City airport, destination Havana, sweat pouring down my neck. Fear—and heat. Nights of terror on New York City streets. Buildings dimming in and out of focus. Waking in the middle of the night dizzy, sick. Anything for the sound of just one human voice to pull myself back. Just one human voice calling, "Susan." Calling my name.

But even those events were simple compared to this one

uncomplicated task—to put one foot in front of the other and slowly cross a plain wooden threshold and look two old people, my parents, in the face.

Their apartment, clean, ordered, showing signs of decay. Not in age—everything new, spotless: the multitude of painted flowers over the white brick fireplace; the seven potted plants each in its own particular space; the arrangement of ashtray (silver), cigarette lighter (silver), picture frame (silver) on a black enamel table. Not in age, in meaning. Everything rising to and resting finally, rootless, on the surface.

A house resting on the surface of things, tied to nothing, growing old.

In the Forties, Fifties, Los Angeles with its trappings of glamour, its obsession with plastic and what is large, had seemed to represent the future—America's as well as mine. But now even that was gone. It was calm, flat, with the dullness of a person grown old in emptiness, with money but without resources, imagination, wonder.

My next stop Berkeley, unlike Los Angeles, was a place I approached with love, not fear. I looked forward to once again walking streets that had changed so much in my life. I saw myself sitting in favorite cafes, movie theaters, one particular spot on the wide university lawns. A remembering surrounded by detail—sights, smells, sounds. A tangible reconstruction of the past.

And I remembered nothing. Recognized nothing. Was thrown into a strange, an alien environment. The magic, once again, in my memory alone. The rest gone cold for me. The years gone cold.

If, by some miracle, I were to suddenly, mysteriously, confront myself fifteen years before, walking down those streets, is it possible I would not have recognized myself? That I would be an absolute stranger to myself as I was then, in the same way that self might not recognize me as I am today?

Almost four decades have passed since this book was lived. Now six years into a new millennium, the United States military is in Iraq. In the name of democracy, over 100,000 Iraqi citizens have been killed, over 3,000 Americans killed, thousands more injured. George W. Bush has been re-elected in another questionable election. Struggles have emerged around globalism, the environment, and digital technology. Racism, sexism, homophobia, economic exploitation continue to be on-going struggles, and I wonder, like so many others, how much was really accomplished during those years of struggle and exploration, how much has really changed.

When people speak of that complexity that was the Sixties they often refer to only one year, 1968. The year of the assassinations of Martin Luther King and Robert Kennedy. The year of the Chicago convention. But no matter how important, one year is not a decade. More than one year, more even than one decade, if one is forced to place parentheses around an era, the period we know as the Sixties really began in the Fifties with the civil rights movement and lasted until the middle Seventies with the end of the Vietnam War.

But, most important, the Sixties was not an isolated era, it was part of a historical continuum of struggle and cultural regeneration, moving backwards, to name only a few political struggles, through the civil rights movement in the Fifties, the progressive movements during the great depression, the labor movement, the first meeting of the NAACP in 1909 to the untold heroic acts against slavery before and during the Civil War to the revolutionary movement out of which this country was born.

Therefore, to label the Sixties a failure or, for that matter, a success, is to ignore its integral place in that continuum that runs not only backward in time but forward through the Seventies, Eighties, Nineties to the present day. What was notable about the Sixties was the numbers of people involved, particularly young people, who rejected the rise of consumerism, political repression and apathy and oppressive puritanism, and began to *live* their difference.

Neither a media-hyped version of a generation dominated by "sex, drugs, and rock & roll" nor an emotionally detached academic study, the real story of the Sixties is how so many of us, each in our own way, faced with the brutal realities exposed by the civil rights movement and the Vietnam War, tried to live out those ideals we had been taught as children. The American dream that had been taught us might be, in the words of Langston Hughes, "a dream deferred," but it was our dream nonetheless. We were, after all, America's children.

In 1990, when I visited East Lansing, Michigan, Diane Wakoski, whom I hadn't seen in many years, described her impression of me at Berkeley as someone "lost." I find that ironic because it was precisely during those years at Berkeley that I came to understand where I belonged. From encountering first love, both revelatory and terrifying, to gathering collectively with students protesting police brutality after the HUAC "police riots," to standing with Ward and our friends against the racism and violence of a gang of teenagers from Oakland, I experienced a sense of connection, of communal support and nurturance, that would grow as the Sixties progressed.

As the poets at the Deux Megots had taught me how to channel my passion into words that could translate the world into something I could grow into and beyond, my experiences in the movement enabled me to transcend my personal struggle with childhood and family through experiencing myself as an integral part of a larger family—that interdependence which was at the heart of an era, that formed the basis of our conviction that we could and would change our world.

But in another way, she was right. There was something missing, something I was searching for, trying desperately to find. Something I could neither name nor identify.

On my wall I have tacked up a reproduction of an old tarot card from Papus' *Tarot of the Bohemians,* one of the few books that translates the first card of the tarot deck, "Le Bateleur," as the juggler rather than as the "magus" or magician. Where the card called the Wheel of Fortune shows the linear sequence of change, the juggler holds all things in balance, holds multiplicity as one. It is that symbol that I use as a guide.

And as I contemplate "The Juggler," my search for home, for myself, for that other who is also me, comes full circle.

New York, 2004. Hurrying home from the theater and my memories of Cuba and the film, *The Control Room,* I have just seen, present and past collide and merge. In the encroaching evening dusk, I can almost imagine myself nineteen again, hurrying down Telegraph Avenue, 1959, the buildings not so different from the tenements lining Sixth Street between First and Second Avenues where I now live. Passing the tiny Mexican restaurant on the corner of Haste and Telegraph where I frequently ate, the equally small cinema another half-block, on to the first-floor grocery store, up the stairs, and into the sanctuary of my Berkeley rooms. I still have no clear picture of the young woman who inhabited them. Wondering again what, if anything, we would have to say to each other, if such a meeting were possible.

And today, late September 2006, as I once more rummage for my keys to open the door fronting East Sixth Street, home at last, I understand at long last that this book *is* our imagined conversation, the intersection of the present and the past.

I understand that what was missing could not be found in my parents' house, no longer my home, in that house empty of everything except memories; could not be found in Berkeley, in Cuba, not even here, in my present home, in New York; could only be found in my own being, the cells of my own body, my own mind. The threshold which takes real courage to cross. Not in retreat, barricaded, but going forward, recapturing meaning, wresting it from the violence that conceals it.

ACKNOWLEDGEMENTS

My gratitude for a Puffin Foundation Grant, a New York Foundation for the Arts Fellowship in Creative Nonfiction Literature, and a residency at Blue Mountain Center for providing time and resources to work on this project.

To Marvin Taylor and the Fales Library New York University El Corno Emplumado Archive for my letters to Margaret Randall, and to Reeni Goldin for sharing with me her information on the 5th St. Women's Building. To Ellen Turner for added materials on the building, and to Allen De Loach for his book *The East Side Scene American Poetry, 1960 - 65* which helped me get some of my details and dates in order.

To The Freedom of Information Act for my FBI files. To Paul Pines and Jantje Tielken for their help with this project, and most of all to Judy Doyle and Sandy Taylor for their generosity of spirit as well as practical advice—and for all the years they have devoted to Curbstone Press.

And, finally, to Natasha Prenn, and to Freeman Palmer and Jacqui Lewis, and to all my loving family at Middle Church for their invaluable support; and to Margaret Randall for making most of this book and life possible.

Some of this material has appeared in a different form in *The Color of the Heart: Writing from Struggle & Change 1959 - 1990; IKON; We Stand Our Ground: Three Women, Their Vision, Their Poems; Big Deal; Downtown; The Aquarian; With Anger/With Love.*

Some of the names of people with whom I had personal relationships have been changed to protect their privacy. Some events from my two trips to Cuba have been interlaced to save space. All events and locations are described to the best of my recollection. Few journal notes or photos were taken at the time by movement activists, apart from articles and essays that appeared in print, because of fear of the repercussions of invasive government surveillance.

Poet, playwright, essayist, and editor of *IKON* magazine, SUSAN SHERMAN has had twelve plays produced off-off-Broadway, has published four collections of poetry and the translation of a Cuban play by Pepe Carril, *Shango de Ima* (Doubleday, 1971) which won 11 AUDELCO awards for a 1996 revival staged by the Nuyorican Poets Café. Her awards include a 1997 fellowship from the New York Foundation for the Arts (NYFA) for Creative Nonfiction Literature, a 1990 NYFA fellowship for Poetry, a Puffin Foundation Grant (1992), a Creative Artists' Public Service (CAPS) poetry grant and editors' awards from the Coordinating Council of Literary Magazines (CCLM) and the New York State Council on the Arts (NYSCA).

Among other periodicals and anthologies, her work has been published in *Changer L'Amérique: Anthologie de la Poésie Protestataire des USA (1980-1995), The Arc of Love, An Ear to the Ground, Poetry (Chicago), The American Poetry Review, The Nation, Conditions, A Gathering of the Tribes, El Corno Emplumado,* and *Heresies.*

She is currently working on *Nirvana on Ninth Street,* a collection of short fiction, and *The Light That Puts an End to Dreams: The "Triumph" of Sor Juana Inés de la Cruz,* an interactive DVD. She is a member of the faculty of Parsons School of Design and Eugene Lang College in New York City.

photo of author: Colleen McKay

Curbstone Press, Inc.
is a non-profit publishing house dedicated to multicultural literature
that reflects a commitment to social awareness and change, with an
emphasis on contemporary writing from Latino, Latin American,
and Vietnamese cultures.

Curbstone's mission focuses on publishing creative writers whose work
promotes human rights and intercultural understanding, and on
bringing these writers and the issues they illuminate into the
community. Curbstone builds bridges between its writers and the
public—from inner-city to rural areas, colleges to cultural centers,
children to adults, with a particular interest in underfunded public
schools. This involves enriching school curricula, reaching out to
underserved audiences by donating books and conducting readings
and educational programs, and promoting discussion in the media.
It is only through these combined efforts that literature can truly
make a difference.

Curbstone Press, like all non-profit presses, relies heavily on the
support of individuals, foundations, and government agencies to bring
you, the reader, works of literary merit and social significance that
would likely not find a place in profit-driven publishing channels, and
to bring these authors and their books into communities across
the country.

If you wish to become a supporter of a specific book—one that is
already published or one that is about to be published—your
contribution will support not only the book's publication but also its
continuation through reprints.

We invite you to support Curbstone's efforts to present the diverse
voices and views that make our culture richer. Tax-deductible
donations can be made to:
Curbstone Press, 321 Jackson Street, Willimantic, CT 06226
phone: (860) 423-5110   fax: (860) 423-9242
www.curbstone.org